CONTENTS.

INTRODUCTION.

Congratulations! You have a book which will inspire you to try out some really exciting recipes on the pages which follow. Every home should have a recipe book devoted entirely to chocolate and this is definitely the one to own. The seductive recipes are easy to follow and are so varied there is one for every occasion, including some delicious gift ideas. Some are quick and simple and are ideal for children to help with making, others are a little more complicated and will need extra care and preparation, but the end result is definitely worth it!

The origins of chocolate are rooted in centuries of history and its earliest documented use was around 1100 BC. It was originally used for making beverages which were served at weddings and funerals. Chocolate first appeared in the Oxford English Dictionary in 1604 and fifty-five years later, in 1659, it was mentioned again and was then referred to as a confection. Today, chocolate has become one of the most popular food types and flavours in the world. It boasts health benefits, such as lowering blood pressure and raising serotonin levels which results in that feel-good-factor that we all want to indulge. There are also claims that it is a third more effective than leading cough-medicine brands.

The great thing about chocolate is its versatility — dark, milk or white chocolate all blend so well with a variety of flavours. Always choose the best quality chocolate you can afford and check the cocoa content to make sure that the chocolate you buy is the best kind for the recipe you are going to follow.

When melting chocolate, always put it into a heatproof bowl over a saucepan of gently simmering water (bain marie), but don't let the bowl touch the water. Warm it through slowly and carefully, or the chocolate may become lumpy and grainy if overheated. When melting chocolate, make sure you stir continuously. If it does overheat, stirring in a small amount of butter may help to restore its smoothness. Always warm any liquid you are about to add to melted chocolate (cream, liqueur, etc.), as cold liquids will cause it to thicken or curdle.

We hope you will get as much pleasure from making these heavenly delicacies as eating them and what better way to unwrap this celebration than with the utmost luxury — a chocolate cake. The recipes which follow in the Cakes and Bakes section are ideal when something is needed for a family tea, or for when friends pop in. They can be made in advance and are sure to be crowd pleasers.

The Biscuits and Cookies section is bursting with scrumptious biscuit ideas, from the delicate madeleines to the Italian biscotti and the more robust oatmeal cookies. An ideal accompaniment to a well-deserved tea-break is bound to restore body and soul.

At any special meal, whether it is in a restaurant, or at a friend's dinner party, don't you always hope there is a chocolate pudding on the menu? The Desserts section contains mouth-watering recipes which will guarantee that your dinner party will be unsurpassed. The variety here offers such flexibility; some deserts can be made in advance and others just before your guests are ready to eat them, but ensure you make plenty, there will be requests for seconds!

Cupcakes and Fancies are the ultimate tea-time treat and afternoon tea with special friends and family would be incomplete without them. It is also becoming increasingly popular to serve these delectable little

cook's choice.
CHOCOLATE

Over 100 mouth-watering recipes

igloobooks

igloobooks

Published in 2014
by Igloo Books Ltd
Cottage Farm
Sywell
NN6 0BJ
www.igloobooks.com

OCE001 0314
2 4 6 8 10 9 7 5 3
ISBN: 978-1-78197-606-7

Food photography and recipe development: Stockfood, The Food Image Agency
Front and back cover images © Stockfood, The Food Image Agency

Printed and manufactured in China.

cakes at weddings and christenings. The recipes here will guarantee to impress even the most discerning of your foodie friends. Why not serve the petit fours or truffles with coffee after a truly dazzling meal?

There are so many occasions which would benefit from the recipes in this book. Chocolate kisses and filled chocolate hearts for Valentine's Day, Christmas petit fours and mini Christmas puddings, chocolate birthday cakes, stelzen marzipan cake at Easter, white chocolate cherries and truffles for parties, along with some beautifully decorated cup-cakes, to name but a few.

Whether you are entertaining family and friends, or having a night in on your own, the delicious recipes in this book will definitely delight. From the sublime stracciatella mousse, to delicious truffles, you can always indulge with heavenly chocolate!

CAKES &
BAKES.

Chocolate cake

Prep and cook time: 1 hour * Cooling time: 1 hour * Cannot be frozen * Serves: 10 - 12

INGREDIENTS:

4 eggs
250 g | 9 oz | 1 ¼ cup sugar
200 ml | 7 fl oz | ⅞ cup vegetable oil
200 ml | 7 fl oz | ⅞ cup orange juice
300 g | 11 oz | 2 ½ cups plain|all
purpose flour
4 tbsp cocoa
1 tsp baking powder
4 cl | 3 tbsp rum, to drizzle
250 ml | 9 fl oz | 1 cup cream
500 g | 18 oz dark chocolate,
70% cocoa

To garnish:
chocolate rolls, 70% cocoa

Also:
butter and flour for the pan

METHOD:

Heat the oven to 200°C (180°C fan) 400°F, gas 6.

Grease the 23 cm - 24 cm | 9 in - 10 in cake pan and dust with flour.

Beat together the eggs and sugar until thick and creamy then
add the oil, orange juice, flour, cocoa and baking powder
and combine.

Pour the mixture into the cake pan, spread smooth and bake for
40 - 45 minutes,

Remove the cake from the oven, remove from the pan and allow to
cool on a wire rack.

Slice horizontally through the middle and drizzle both halves
with rum.

To ice the cake, bring the cream to a boil and pour over the
chocolate. Stir until smooth and let cool to room temperature.

Spread the cake halves with about ⅓ of the chocolate and
reassemble. Ice the cake all over using the remaining chocolate and
decorate with chocolate rolls.

White chocolate layer cake

Prep and cook time: 1 hour * Chill: 12 hours * Can be frozen * Serves: 6-8

INGREDIENTS:

120 g | 4 oz | 1 cup flour
80 g | 3 oz | ¾ stick cold butter
2 tbsp cocoa powder
3 tbsp sugar
1 pinch salt
1 egg yolk
100 g | 3 ½ oz | ⅓ cup apricot jam
300 g | 11 oz white cooking chocolate
125 g | 4 ½ oz | ½ cup whipping cream
1 vanilla pod
2 cl | 1 ½ tbsp rum
150 g | 5 oz | 1 ½ sticks butter

METHOD:

Heat the oven to 180°C (160°C fan) 350°F, gas 5.

Combine the flour, butter, cocoa powder, sugar, salt and egg yolk and work to into a pliable dough.

Form into a ball, wrap in cling film and put into the refrigerator for 30 minutes.

Roll out on a floured work surface to a thickness of 3 mm / ⅛".

Cut out 5 rectangles measuring 12 x 6 cm / 5 x 2 ½". (Reroll the pastry scraps and cut more rectangles until you have enough).

Put the rectangles on a cookie sheet lined with baking parchment and bake in a preheated oven (180°C/350°F, middle shelf) for about 15 minutes. Take out and cool on a cake rack, then spread with the apricot jam.

Melted the chopped chocolate in a bowl over a pan of simmering water.

Put the cream into a pan with the vanilla seeds and bring to a boil. Mix with the melted chocolate and rum and leave to cool.

Cream the butter and mix with the cooled chocolate cream. Chill for 30 minutes.

Line a 1 kg | 2 lb loaf tin with cling film and fill with alternate layers of chocolate cream and baked chocolate rectangles. Cover and chill overnight.

Chocolate orange loaf

Prep and cook time: 1 hour * Can be frozen * Serves: 6-8

INGREDIENTS:

70 g | 2 ½ oz dark chocolate, 70% cocoa
6 eggs, separated
1 pinch salt
200 g | 7 oz | 2 cups finely ground almonds
60 g | 2 oz | ⅓ cup cane sugar
125 g | 4 ½ oz | ⅔ cup sugar
1 untreated orange, grated zest and juice
6 cl | 4 tbsp orange liqueur
100 g | 3 ½ oz | ¾ cup plain|all purpose flour
3 tbsp cornflour|cornstarch
½ tsp vanilla extract
50 g | 1 ¾ oz | ⅓ cup almond flakes
icing|confectioners' sugar to dust
butter and flour for the pan

METHOD:

Heat the oven to 200°C (180°C fan) 400°F, gas 6.

Brush the 1 kg | 2 lb loaf pan with butter and dust with flour.

Beat the egg whites with the salt until very stiff.

Lightly toast the almonds without fat in a skillet and let cool.

Beat the egg yolks with the cane sugar, sugar and orange zest to a creamy consistency. Continue beating, slowly adding the liqueur and orange juice.

Fold in the ground almonds, flour, cornflour/cornstarch and vanilla extract.

Fold in the beaten egg whites and grated chocolate.

Pour the batter into the loaf pan, scatter with flaked almonds and bake for 50 minutes.

Leave to cool in the pan, tip out the loaf, cut and serve dusted with icing/confectioners' sugar.

Chocolate banana dome cake

Prep and cook time: 50 minutes ∗ Chill: 4 hours ∗ Cannot be frozen ∗ Serves: 10 - 12

INGREDIENTS:

For the sponge cake:
5 eggs, separated
125 g | 4 ½ oz | 1 ¼ cups
icing|confectioners' sugar
40 g | 1 ½ oz | ⅓ cup plain|
all purpose flour
50 g | 1 ¾ oz | ½ cup cornflour|cornstarch
30 g | 1 oz | 3 tbsp cocoa powder

For the filling:
2 cl | 1 ½ tbsp brandy
2 cl | 1 ½ tbsp almond liqueur
6 leaves of gelatine, soaked
in cold water
350 g | 12 oz dark chocolate,
70% cocoa
1000 ml | 35 fl oz | 4 cups cream
50 g | 1 ¾ oz | ½ cup icing|confectioners'
sugar
2 large bananas
2 tbsp lemon juice

To decorate:
chocolate hearts, good quality white
chocolate and dark chocolate
(70% cocoa)
chocolate curls
icing|confectioners' sugar to dust

METHOD:

Heat the oven to 220°C (200°C fan) 425°F, gas 7 and line two large cookie sheets with baking parchment.

To make the batter, beat the egg yolks and icing/confectioner's sugar until creamy. Beat the egg whites until forming very stiff peaks and fold into the egg yolks. Sieve the flour, cornflour/cornstarch and cocoa onto the eggs and fold in.

Spread the batter on the cookie sheets about 0.5" thick to form one circle of about 9.5" diameter and one circle of about 12.5 " diameter. Bake for 10-15 minutes.

Turn the sponge cakes out onto cooling racks, peel off the baking parchment, cover and allow to cool.

Line a shallow rounded bowl (capacity approximately 1 ltr / 2 quarts) with cling film. Place the larger sponge cake circle in the bowl and brush with a mixture of brandy and almond liqueur.

Soak the gelatine sheets in water. Melt the chocolate with 100 ml cream over simmering water, squeeze the gelatine to remove excess water and dissolve in the hot chocolate. Remove from the heat and let cool slightly.

Whip the remaining cream with the icing/confectioners' sugar until very stiff and fold into the cooled melted chocolate.

Peel the bananas, slice and drizzle with lemon juice.

Spoon ⅔ of the filling into the sponge bowl, cover with the sliced banana and place the smaller sponge cake circle on top. Chill for 2 hours.

Turn the cake onto a plate, remove the cling film and spread with the remaining chocolate mixture. Decorate with chocolate curls and hearts and chill for a further 2 hours.

Serve dusted with icing/confectioners' sugar and cut into slices.

Coffee and chocolate marble cake with meringue

Prep and cook time: 1 hour 30 minutes * Cannot be frozen * Serves: 10 - 12

INGREDIENTS:

125 g | 4 ½ oz dark chocolate, 70% cocoa
250 ml | 9 fl oz | 1 cup espresso
4 cl | 3 tbsp coffee liqueur
200 g | 7 oz | 2 sticks butter
175 g | 6 oz | ¾ cup sugar
1 tsp vanilla extract
4 eggs
250 g | 9 oz | 2 ½ cups plain| all purpose flour
1 tsp baking powder
75 ml | 2 ½ fl oz | ⅓ cup milk

For the meringue topping:
2 egg whites
50 g | 1 ¾ oz | ¼ cup sugar

METHOD:

Heat the oven to 180°C (160°C fan) 375°F, gas 5.

Melt the chocolate in a bowl over simmering water, together with the espresso and the coffee liqueur.

Beat the butter, sugar and vanilla extract until light and creamy.

Remove from the heat and beat in the eggs, one at a time.

Stir in the flour and the baking powder and add some milk until the batter is smooth.

Pour about ⅓ of the batter into another bowl and stir in the melted chocolate.

Pour the chocolate batter into a buttered 1 kg | 2 lb loaf tin.

Spread some of the chocolate batter up the sides of the loaf tin.

Pour the vanilla batter over the top and level the top.

Bake for 60 minutes. Test with a wooden toothpick, if it comes out clean, it can be removed from the oven. If it starts to get too brown, cover with a piece of tin foil.

To make the meringue topping, whisk the egg whites until stiff. Slowly add the sugar and continue whisking.

Remove the cake from the oven. Spread the meringue over the top and place under the grill, or back in the over for 4 - 5 minutes to brown.

Gently turn the cake out of the loaf pan and let cool.

Chocolate refrigerator cake

Prep and cook time: 1 hour 30 minutes * Chill: 3 hours * Cannot be frozen * Serves: 8 - 10

INGREDIENTS:

100 g | 3 ½ oz dark chocolate,
70% cocoa
125 g | 4 ½ oz | 1 ¼ sticks butter
75 g | 2 ½ oz | ¾ cup icing|confectioners'
sugar
40 g | 1 ½ oz | ½ cup finely
ground almonds
2 - 3 tbsp cocoa liqueur
300 g | 11 oz shortbread cookies
cocoa powder to dust

METHOD:

Melt the chocolate and butter in a pan over a low heat,
stirring constantly.

Mix in the icing/confectioners' sugar, almonds and cocoa liqueur
and allow to cool slightly.

Spoon half of the chocolate butter into a 23 cm | 9 in spring form
pan lined with cling film.

One by one, press the cookies vertically into the chocolate butter
going round in concentric circles and ensuring that the cookies touch
the bottom of the pan.

Spoon the remaining chocolate butter between the cookies to fill
any gaps.

Chill for at least 3 hours then remove the cake from the pan and
peel off the cling film.

Cut the cake into slices (easiest with a hot knife) and serve dusted
with cocoa powder.

Chocolate fudge cake

Prep and cook time: 1 hour 10 minutes ∗ Cannot be frozen ∗ Serves: 8 - 10

INGREDIENTS:

For the batter:
125 g | 4 ½ oz dark chocolate
2 tbsp orange liqueur
4 eggs, separated
1 pinch salt
135 g | 5 oz | ⅔ cup sugar
125 g | 4 ½ oz | 1 ¼ stick butter, softened
2 tbsp maple syrup
100 g | 3 ½ oz | 1 cup ground hazelnuts
35 g | 1 ¼ oz | ⅓ cup coconut flakes
4 - 6 soft caramel candies, chopped

For the fudge:
400 g | 14 oz | 2 cups sugar
50 g | 1 ¾ oz | ⅔ cup cocoa powder
235 ml | 8 fl oz | 1 cup milk
60 ml | 2 fl oz | ¼ cup melted butter
2 tsp vanilla extract

METHOD:

Heat the oven to 175°C (160°C fan) 350°F, gas 4.

Melt the chocolate with the liqueur over simmering water.

Beat the egg whites until stiff with a pinch of salt, gradually add 3 tbsp of sugar and continue beating until firm and glossy.

Cream the butter with the rest of the sugar until pale and creamy. Stir the egg yolks, maple syrup and chocolate into the butter. Fold in the beaten egg whites, ground hazelnuts and coconut flakes.

Grease a 15 cm x 30 cm | 6 in x 12 in baking tin and sprinkle with flour.

Fold the caramel candies into the batter.

Turn the batter into the baking tin and bake for 50 minutes. After 35 minutes, cover the cake with kitchen foil and return to the oven. Remove from the oven and allow to cool on a cooling rack.

To make the fudge, place the sugar, cocoa powder and milk into a saucepan and bring to a boil, stirring constantly. Reduce the heat, do not stir any further and check the temperature using a sugar thermometer: it should be 114°C / 237°F (alternatively, check by dropping a little bit of the mixture into a cup of cold water – if the fudge forms a soft, malleable lump, it is ready).

Remove from the heat, stir in the butter and the vanilla extract. Beat with a wooden spoon until the fudge becomes matt instead of glossy.

Pour the fudge onto the cake, spread evenly and let cool.

Chocolate raspberry roll

Prep and cook time: 35 minutes * Chill: 3 hours * Cannot be frozen * Serves: 10 - 12

INGREDIENTS:

For the sponge cake:
4 egg whites
125 g | 4 ½ oz | ⅔ cup sugar
4 egg yolks
80 g | 3 oz | ⅗ cup plain|all purpose flour
40 g | 1 ½ oz | ⅓ cup cornflour|cornstarch
40 g | 1 ½ oz | ¼ cup cocoa powder
1 tsp | baking powder
sugar for rolling

For the filling:
400 ml | 14 fl oz | 1 ⅔ cups cream
70 g | 2 ½ oz | ⅓ cup sugar
3 leaves of white gelatine, softened
in cold water
150 g | 5 oz | 1 cup raspberries

METHOD:

Heat the oven to 220°C (200°C fan) 425°F, gas 7 and line a cookie sheet with baking parchment.

Beat the egg whites and 4 tbsp of cold water until you have stiff peaks. Slowly add the sugar and stir.

Fold the egg yolks into the egg white mixture.

Mix together the flour, cornflour/cornstarch, cocoa powder and baking powder and sieve into the egg whites.

Spread the mixture onto the cookie sheet and bake for around 12 minutes. Allow to cool for 5 minutes, then invert onto a dish towel sprinkled with sugar. Carefully peel off the baking parchment, roll up and let cool.

To make the filling, whip the cream and sugar until stiff.

Place the wet gelatine in a pan and dissolve over a low heat. Stir about 3 tbsp of cream into the gelatine then mix well with the rest of the cream.

Unroll the sponge cake, spread with the cream and scatter with raspberries.

Roll up and chill in the refrigerator for at least 3 hours. Serve dusted with icing/confectioners' sugar.

Chocolate fridge cake

Prep and cook time: 30 minutes * Chill: 4 hours * Cannot be frozen * Serves: 6-8

INGREDIENTS:

600 g | 21 oz dark chocolate
150 g | 5 oz | ¾ cup coconut oil
200 ml | 7 fl oz | ⅞ cup cream
100 g | 3 ½ oz | ½ cup
chopped almonds
250 g | 9 oz | 2 cups shortbread cookies

METHOD:

Melt the chocolate with the coconut oil and cream over simmering water, stirring constantly.

Remove from the heat, stir in the nuts and allow to cool slightly.

Line the 1.5 litre | 3 lb loaf pan with cling film.

Spoon a little chocolate into the pan and cover with cookies. Continue to layer up chocolate and cookies until all ingredients are used up. Chill for at least 4 hours.

To serve, turn out of the pan, remove the cling film and cut into slices.

Mini chocolate espresso cakes

Prep and cook time: 40 minutes * Cannot be frozen * Serves: 6

INGREDIENTS:

125 g | 4 ½ oz | 1 ¼ sticks butter, room temperature
100 g | 3 ½ oz | ½ cup sugar
1 pinch of salt
3 eggs
250 g | 9 oz | 2 cups spelt flour
2 tbsp cocoa powder
2 tsp baking powder
2 tsp instant coffee
150 ml | 5 fl oz | ⅔ cup skim milk
butter and flour for the cake pans
cocoa powder to dust

METHOD:

Heat the oven to 200°C (180°C fan) 400°F, gas 6.

Cream the butter, sugar and salt until light and fluffy. Add the eggs and beat until the mixture is pale and creamy.

Mix the flour, cocoa, baking powder and instant coffee and add to the egg mixture with the milk. Mix to a soft consistency, adding a little more milk if it is too stiff.

Butter 6 x 10 cm | 4 in small bundt pans and dust with flour. Divide the mixture between the tins and bake for 25 - 30 minutes, until golden brown. Leave to cool completely.

Serve the cakes dusted with cocoa.

Chocolate loaf

Prep and cook time: 35 minutes * Baking time: 1 hour * Cannot be frozen * Serves: 4-6

INGREDIENTS:

For the sponge cake:

200 g | 7 oz dark chocolate, 70% cocoa
200 g | 7 oz | 2 sticks butter, softened
150 g | 5 oz | 1 ½ cups icing|confectioners'
sugar
8 eggs, separated
100 g | 3 ½ oz | ½ cup sugar
150 g | 5 oz | 1 1/4 cups plain|
all purpose flour
50 g | 1 ¾ oz | ½ cup finely
ground almonds

For the frosting:

150 g | 5 oz dark chocolate, 70% cocoa

Also:

butter to grease the pan

METHOD:

Heat the oven to 180°C (160°C fan) 375°F, gas 5.

Grease the 1.2 litre | 3 lb loaf pan and scatter with ground almonds. Tap the tin and save any excess almonds.

To make the sponge, melt ¾ of the chocolate over simmering water and let cool.

Cream together the butter and icing/confectioner's sugar.

Add the egg yolks with the melted chocolate a little at a time, to the butter mixture and stir in.

Beat the egg whites and sugar until stiff and fold carefully into the chocolate mixture.

Mix the flour with the remaining almonds and chocolate and fold into the mixture.

Pour the batter into the loaf pan and bake for 1 hour. Remove from the oven, allow to cool for 5 minutes. Remove from the loaf tin and leave to cool completely.

To frost the cake, melt the chocolate over simmering water and let cool. Pour over the cake.

Chocolate triangles with mint and cream

Prep and cook time: 45 minutes ∗ Chill: 4 hours ∗ Cannot be frozen ∗ Makes: 10 - 12

INGREDIENTS:

For the sponge cake:
8 eggs, separated
150 g | 5 oz | ⅘ cup sugar
1 pinch salt
1 tsp lemon zest, finely grated
160 g | 6 oz | 1 ¼ cup plain|all purpose flour
50 g | 1 ¾ oz | ½ cup cornflour|cornstarch
50 g | 1 ¾ oz | ⅓ cup cocoa powder

For the filling:
6 leaves of gelatine
250 g | 9 oz | 1 cup quark
250 g | 9 oz | 1 cup cream cheese
200 ml | 7 fl oz | ⅞ cup cream
50 g | 1 ¾ oz | ½ cup icing|confectioners' sugar
100 g | 3 ½ oz chocolate with mint filling, chopped

To garnish:
50 ml | 1 ¾ fl oz | 10 tsp cream
chocolate with mint filling
cocoa to dust

METHOD:

Heat the oven to 240°C (220°C fan) 475°F, gas 9 and line a 35 cm x 25 cm | 14 in x 10 in cookie sheet with baking parchment.

Beat the egg yolks with the salt, lemon zest and half the sugar to a smooth consistency.

Beat the egg whites with the remaining sugar until stiff and fold in the egg yolk mixture.

Sieve the flour, cornflour/cornstarch and cocoa over the bowl and slowly fold into the eggs.

Spread the sponge cake mixture evenly onto the cookie sheet and bake for 10 minutes.

Invert the sponge cake onto a dish towel scattered with sugar, peel off the parchment and let cool.

Mix the quark and cream cheese together until smooth.

Squeeze the excess water from the gelatine and melt slowly in a pan.

Stir 2 tbsp of the quark mixture into the gelatine. Stir the gelatine mixture into the quark and cream cheese.

Whip the cream and icing/confectioners' sugar until stiff and stir into the quark along with the mint chocolate.

Cut the sponge cake into two halves. Spread one half with the quark mixture, place the other sponge cake half on top and press down carefully.

Chill for at least 3 hours then cut into triangles.

To serve, whip the cream until stiff. Garnish each triangle with cream and mint chocolate and dust with cocoa.

Chocolate banana cake

Prep and cook time: 50 minutes * Cannot be frozen * Serves: 4 - 6

INGREDIENTS:

250 g | 9 oz | 2 ¼ cups plain|all
purpose flour
100 g | 3 ½ oz | ½ cup sugar
2 tbsp soy flour
3 tsp baking powder
3 - 4 tbsp dark cocoa powder
250 ml | 9 fl oz | 1 cup soy milk
80 ml | 3 fl oz | ⅓ cup oil
4 tbsp water
2 bananas

METHOD:

Heat the oven to 180°C (160°C fan) 350°F, gas 5.

Oil and chill a 1 kg | 2 lb loaf tin.

Put all the flour, sugar, soy flour, baking powder and cocoa powder
into a bowl and mix together.

Mix all the wet ingredients in a separate bowl and quickly mix in the
dry ingredients.

Peel the bananas, halve lengthways and cut into pieces. Fold into
the batter.

Spread the batter evenly in the loaf tin and bake for
30 - 40 minutes.

Test by inserting a wooden toothpick, if it comes out clean,
it is ready. Let the loaf cool slightly before turning out onto
a cooling rack.

Nutty millionaires' shortbread

Prep and cook time: 50 minutes * Cannot be frozen * Makes: 18 - 20

INGREDIENTS:

For the shortbread:
225 g | 8 oz | 2 sticks butter
100 g | 3 ½ oz | ½ cup sugar
1 egg yolk
275 g | 10 oz | 2 cups plain|all purpose flour

For the caramel:
125 g | 4 ½ oz | 1 ¼ stick butter
125 g | 4 ½ oz | 10 tbsp sugar
400 g | 14 oz | 2 cups
evaporated milk
60 g | 2 oz | 3 tbsp honey
150 g | 5 oz | 1 cup peanuts, chopped

For the topping:
230 g | 8 oz dark chocolate
2 tbsp coconut oil

METHOD:

Heat the oven to 200°C (180°C fan) 400°F, gas 6.

To make the shortbread, cream together the butter, sugar and egg yolk, sieve in the flour and combine to form a smooth dough.

Tip the dough into the 20 cm | 8 in square cake pan, press down firmly and bake for 25 minutes. Remove from the oven and allow to cool.

To make the caramel, heat the butter and add the sugar and evaporated milk.

Stir in the honey and bring to a boil. Simmer for 6 - 8 minutes, stirring constantly, until the mixture caramelizes in the pan becomes golden brown and thick. Stir in the peanuts.

Pour the caramel over the shortbread, smooth with an oiled dough scraper and allow to cool.

To make the topping, melt the chocolate over simmering water and let cool slightly.

When the caramel is almost solid, pour over the chocolate and allow to cool.

Remove from the cake pan. Before the chocolate and caramel have set solid, cut into small squares.

Raspberry cheesecake slices

Prep and cook time: 45 minutes * Chill: 4 hours * Cannot be frozen * Makes: 18 - 20

INGREDIENTS:

For the base:
400 g | 14 oz | 3 1/3 cups
chocolate cookies
100 g | 3 1/2 oz | 1 stick butter, melted

For the topping:
500 g | 18 oz | 3 1/2 cups
raspberries, sorted
500 g | 18 oz | 2 1/2 cups quark
(low-fat soft cheese)
500 g | 18 oz | 2 1/2 cups mascarpone
200 g | 7 oz | 1 1/2 cups yoghurt
1 lemon, juice and finely grated zest
250 ml | 9 fl oz | 1 cup cream
150 g | 5 oz | 3/4 cup sugar
4 cl | 2 1/2 tbsp raspberry brandy
15 leaves of gelatine, soaked in
cold water

METHOD:

Crumble the chocolate cookies and mix with melted butter.

Spread the cookie mixture onto a 30 cm x 40 cm | 12 in x 16 in baking pan lined with baking parchment and press down firmly. Chill for 30 minutes.

Puree 1/3 of the raspberries and push through a sieve. Scatter the remaining raspberries on the cookie base.

Beat together the quark, mascarpone, yoghurt, lemon juice, lemon zest and sugar until smooth and creamy.

Squeeze the gelatine to remove excess water. Warm the raspberry brandy, dissolve the leaves of gelatine in it and quickly mix into the quark mixture.

Place half the quark mixture in another bowl and stir in the raspberry puree. Return the raspberry quark to the main bowl and mix lightly to achieve a marbled effect.

Pour onto the cookie base, spread smooth and chill for at least 4 hours until firmly set.

Cut into equal slices and serve.

Cherry choc brownies

Prep and cook time: 40 minutes * Can be frozen * Makes: 20

INGREDIENTS:

For the brownies:
200 g | 7 oz chocolate, 70% cocoa
200 g | 7 oz | 1 ¾ sticks butter
4 eggs, separated
200 g | 7 oz | 1 cup sugar
100 g | 3 ½ oz | ¾ cup plain|all purpose flour

For the cherry sauce:
1 jar Morello cherries
1 tsp sugar
1 good pinch ground cinnamon
1 tbsp potato starch flour

METHOD:

Heat the oven to 210°C (190°C fan) 410°F, gas 6.

Butter a 34 cm x 24 cm | 13 ½ in x 10 in baking tin.

Melt the chocolate over simmering water, then remove from the heat and stir in the cold butter, a few pieces at a time until creamy.

Beat the egg whites until stiff.

Beat the egg yolks with the sugar until pale, thick and creamy.

Carefully stir the egg yolk mixture into the cooled chocolate and butter mixture then fold in the beaten egg whites.

Sieve the flour over the mixture and carefully fold in.

Turn the mixture into the greased tin and bake for 20 minutes. Leave to cool in the tin.

For the cherry sauce, put the cherries into a saucepan with their juice (keeping back 3 tablespoons), add the sugar and heat gently.

Put the cinnamon, potato starch flour and the 3 tablespoons of cherry juice into a cup and mix to a smooth paste. Then stir into the cherries, bring briefly to a boil and remove from the heat.

Cut the cake into 10 squares and then into triangles.

Pour over the cherry sauce to serve.

Chocolate nut brownies

Prep and cook time: 1 hour ∗ Cooling time: 3 hours ∗ Cannot be frozen ∗ Makes: 25

INGREDIENTS:

250 g | 9 oz | 2 ¼ sticks butter, softened
150 g | 5 oz | ¾ cup sugar
4 eggs
200 g | 7 oz dark chocolate, grated
250 g | 9 oz | 2 ½ cups ground hazelnuts
(cob nuts)
250 g | 9 oz | 2 cups plain|all purpose flour
½ tsp baking powder
½ tsp cinnamon
1 tbsp cocoa powder

For the topping:
250 g | 9 oz | 2 ¼ sticks butter
250 g | 9 oz | 1 ¼ cups sugar
800 g | 28 oz condensed milk
120 g | 4 oz | 5 ½ tbsp honey
600 g | 21 oz | 3 ½ cups mixed nuts, (e. g.
hazelnuts (cob nuts), pistachios, almonds,
walnuts), roughly chopped

METHOD:

Heat the oven to 200°C (180°C fan) 400°F, gas 6.

Cream the butter and sugar and beat in the eggs.

Stir the grated chocolate, ground hazelnuts, flour, baking powder, cinnamon and cocoa into the creamed mixture.

Spread the mixture approximately 2 cm thick on a greased 25 cm | 10 in baking tray and bake for 20 - 25 minutes.

To make the topping, warm the butter and add the sugar, condensed milk and honey and bring to the boil.

Simmer and stir for 5 - 10 minutes until caramelized. Fold in the nuts.

Pour over the baked brownie base, spread smoothly and leave to cool.

Cut into small rectangles and serve.

Coffee chocolate slices with vanilla cream and fruit compote

Prep and cook time: 1 hour 30 minutes * Chill: 5 hours * Cannot be frozen * Makes: 12

INGREDIENTS:

For the base:
200 g | 7 oz dark chocolate
100 g | 3 ½ oz coffee flavored chocolate
6 eggs, separated
1 pinch salt
300 g | 11 oz | 1 ½ cups sugar
2 cl | 4 tsp | 1 small cup strong espresso
300 g | 11 oz | 1 ⅓ cups margarine
150 g | 5 oz | 1 ¼ cups plain|
all purpose flour

For the topping:
70 g | 2 ½ oz | ⅔ cup corn
cornflour|cornstarch
100 g | 3 ½ oz | ½ cup sugar
800 ml | 28 fl oz | 3 ½ cups milk
1 vanilla pod
200 g | 7 oz | 2 sticks butter

For the fruit compote:
1 ripe mango, peeled, de-stoned
and chopped
½ papaya, peeled, deseeded and chopped
2 limes, washed, zest finely grated
and juiced
Sugar to taste

To garnish: herbs, e. g. mint

METHOD:

Heat the oven to 180°C (160°C fan) 350°F, gas 5.

To make the base, melt the chocolate over simmering water.

Meanwhile, beat the egg whites with the salt until they form stiff peaks. Beat the egg yolks with the sugar and the espresso until thick and foamy and the sugar has dissolved.

Remove the chocolate from the heat, stir the margarine into it a few small pieces at a time and fold into the egg yolk mixture.

Sift the flour over and fold in with the beaten egg whites.

Turn the batter into a greased and floured 33 cm x 23 cm | 13 in x 9 in baking pan and bake for 25 - 30 minutes.

Meanwhile mix the cornflour/cornstarch and sugar smoothly with a little of the milk. Slit the vanilla pod open and scrape out the seeds. Put the rest of the milk into a pan with the vanilla pod and seeds and bring to a boil.

As soon as the milk boils, remove the pan from the heat and stir in the mixed cornflour/cornstarch. Return to the heat and briefly return to a boil, stirring constantly. Remove from the heat, take out the vanilla pod and allow to cool slightly, while stirring. Gradually stir in the cold butter.

Take the cake out of the oven, let cool slightly then turn out onto a cake plate. Replace the baking pan ring around the cake and spread the vanilla cream smoothly on top of the cake.

Chill the cake for 5 hours.

Place the chopped fruit into a pan with the lime juice and zest. Heat and simmer for 5 minutes. Sweeten to taste. Put into jars, seal well and let cool.

Cut the cake into pieces and serve decorated with a little fruit compote and herbs of your choice.

Rocky road

Prep and cook time: 20 minutes * Chill: 3 hours * Can be frozen * Makes: 12 - 14

INGREDIENTS:

175 g | 6 oz | ½ cup shortbread cookies,
roughly crumbled

300 g | 11 oz dark chocolate, 70% cocoa

100 g | 3 ½ oz milk chocolate

4 tbsp maple syrup

150 g | 5 oz | 1 ½ sticks butter

150 g | 5 oz | 3 cups mini marshmallows,
pink and white

150 g | 5 oz | 1 cup pecan nuts,
coarsely chopped

METHOD:

Melt both chocolates in a pan with the syrup and butter over a low heat stirring constantly and let cool slightly.

Stir in the cookies, marshmallows and nuts and spoon into a cake pan (approximately 8" x 8") lined with cling film.

Chill for at least 3 hours until set solid.

Turn out of the tray, peel of the plastic wrap, cut into pieces and serve.

Stelzen marzipan cake

Prep and cook time: 45 minutes * Cannot be frozen * Makes: 30

INGREDIENTS:

For the sponge cake:
200 g | 7 oz | 2 sticks softened butter
200 g | 7 oz | 1 cup sugar
3 eggs
200 g | 7 oz | 1 ⅗ cups flour
1 tsp baking powder
1 pinch salt
150 g | 5 oz | 1 ¼ cups sour cream
2 tbsp cocoa powder

For the marzipan:
250 g | 9 oz | 2 ½ sticks butter
200 g | 7 oz | 1 ½ cups icing|confectioners'
sugar
250 g | 9 oz | 1 ⅔ cups
semolina|cream of wheat
1 tbsp rum
5 drops bitter almond flavor

For the chocolate frosting:
125 g | 4 ½ oz | ½ cup coconut oil
2 tbsp rum
1 egg
125 g | 4 ½ oz | 1 cup icing|confectioners'
sugar
2 tbsp cocoa powder

To garnish:
hundreds and thousands sugar decorations

METHOD:

Heat the oven to 200°C (180°C fan) 400°F, gas 6.

Line a cookie sheet with baking parchment.

To make the cake mix, beat the butter and sugar to a creamy consistency. Add the eggs little by little and continue beating.

Stir in the flour, baking powder, salt, sour cream and cocoa powder.

Spread the mix on a 30 cm x 40 cm | 12 in x 16 in baking tin, smooth and bake for 25 - 30 minutes in the preheated oven. Remove and let cool.

To make the marzipan, melt the butter, stir in the icing/confectioners' sugar and semolina/cream of wheat and bring briefly to a boil.

Add the rum and almond flavour and immediately spread the mixture onto the cake.

To make the frosting, melt the coconut oil and let cool slightly.

Beat together the rum and egg and mix into the coconut oil along with the icing/confectioners' sugar and cocoa powder. Spread on top of the marzipan.

Scatter with sugar strands and chill until serving.

Raspberry and white chocolate crumble cake

Prep and cook time: 1 hour 15 minutes ∗ Can be frozen ∗ Makes: 20 - 24 slices

INGREDIENTS:

For the batter:
160 g | 6 oz | 1 ½ sticks butter,
room temperature
180 g | 6 oz | ¾ cup 1 tbsp sugar
5 eggs
400 g | 14 oz | 3 cups plain|all purpose flour
2 tsp baking powder

For the topping:
3 - 4 tbsp breadcrumbs
750 g | 26 oz | 5 cups raspberries
200 g | 7 oz white chocolate

For the crumble:
125 g | 4 ½ oz | 1 ¼ sticks
butter, softened
125 g | 4 ½ oz | 1 cup plain|
all purpose flour
75 g | 2 ½ oz | ¾ cup ground almonds
100 g | 3 ½ oz | ½ cup sugar

To serve:
150 ml | 5 fl oz | ⅔ cup cream

METHOD:

Heat the oven to 220°C (200°C fan) 425°F, gas 7.

Combine the butter, sugar, eggs, flour and baking powder to
a smooth batter.

Line a 30 cm x 40 cm | 12 in x 16 in baking pan with baking
parchment, evenly spread out the batter and smooth the surface.

Sprinkle the batter with breadcrumbs. Mix the raspberries and
chopped white chocolate together and distribute evenly across
the surface.

To make the crumble, cut together the butter, flour, almonds and
sugar in a bowl until the mixture resembles breadcrumbs. Scatter
the crumble over the cake.

Bake for 50 minutes. Cover with tin foil if the cake browns
too quickly.

Cut into slices and serve warm with whipped cream.

Chocolate raisin flapjacks

Prep and cook time: 40 minutes * Cannot be frozen * Makes: 10 - 12

INGREDIENTS:

200 g | 7 oz | 2 sticks butter,
100 g | 3 ½ oz | ½ cup cane sugar
2 tbsp maple syrup
275 g | 10 oz | 3 ½ cups rolled oats
40 g | 1 ½ oz | ½ cup cocoa powder
75 g | 2 ½ oz | ½ cup raisins

METHOD:

Heat the oven to 180°C (160°C fan) 375°F, gas 5.

Grease a small, shallow cookie sheet approximately 7"x 7" in size. Alternatively use a regular cookie sheet and make a border of the appropriate size using tin foil.

Melt the butter, sugar and syrup over a low heat. Add the rolled oats and cocoa powder and mix well.

Spread half of the mixture onto the cookie sheet and sprinkle with the raisins. Pour the other half of the flapjack mixture on top of the raisins and spread smooth.

Bake for 30 minutes, allow to cool and cut into about 12 flapjacks.

Millionaires' shortbread

Prep and cook time: 50 minutes * Can be frozen * Makes: 24 pieces

INGREDIENTS:

350 g | 12 oz | 1 ½ cups butter
250 g | 9 oz | 1 ⅓ cups sugar
1 egg
275 g | 10 oz | 2 ½ cups flour
300 ml | 11 fl oz | 1 ⅓ cups condensed milk
60 ml | 2 fl oz | ¼ cup honey
200 g | 7 oz dark chocolate,
min 64% cocoa
30 g | 1 oz | 2 tbsp clarified butter
15 g | ½ oz white chocolate

METHOD:

Heat the oven to 180°C (160°C fan) 350°F, gas 4.

Cream 225 g / 1 cup butter with 100 g / ½ cup sugar until light and fluffy (beat in the egg, if using).

Sieve the flour over and knead to a pliable dough. Press the mixture into a 23 cm x 28 cm | 9 in x 11 in baking tin and smooth the top. Bake for 20 minutes.

For the topping, warm the rest of the butter, add the sugar and allow to caramelize.

Then add the condensed milk, stir in the honey, bring to a boil and simmer for about 20 minutes (or longer if necessary), until the mixture is thick and caramelized.

Pour over the shortbread base and let cool.

Melt the dark chocolate with the clarified butter over a bain marie, pour over the caramel and let cool.

Melt the white chocolate over a bain marie, then put into a small paper bag, snip off one corner and decorate the cake with drizzles of white chocolate. Cut into squares before serving.

Chocolate pistachio slices

Prep and cook time: 40 minutes ∗ Chill: 4 hours ∗ Cannot be frozen ∗ Makes: 10

INGREDIENTS:

For the pastry:
200 g | 7 oz | 1 ½ cups plain|all purpose flour
1 pinch salt
60 g | 2 oz | ⅓ cup sugar
100 g | 3 ½ oz | 1 stick butter
1 egg

For the topping:
160 ml | 6 fl oz | ⅔ cup cream
500 g | 18 oz dark chocolate, 70% cocoa
4 cl | 3 tbsp almond liqueur
150 g | 5 oz | 1 cup pistachio nut kernels, roughly chopped

METHOD:

Heat the oven to 200°C (180°C fan) 400°F, gas 6.

Mix together the flour, salt, sugar, butter and egg to make the pastry dough. Roll out to a rectangular 10 cm x 25 cm | 4 in x 10 in baking tin and pierce the base several times with a fork.

Bake for 25 minutes. Remove from the oven and let cool.

To make the filling, bring the cream to a boil and then slowly pour onto the chocolate with the liqueur, stirring constantly until the mixture is thick and creamy and the chocolate has completely dissolved.

Fold the pistachios into the filling and spread on the pastry base. Smooth and chill for at least 4 hours.

To serve, remove from the baking tin and cut into slices.

Cherry and coconut slices with chocolate frosting

Prep and cook time: 1 hours 30 minutes * Cannot be frozen * Makes: 24

INGREDIENTS:

200 g | 7 oz | 2 cups coconut flakes
400 g | 14 oz | 2 cups sugar
400 g | 14 oz | 3 ½ sticks butter
8 eggs
400 g | 14 oz | 3 ¼ cups plain|all
purpose flour
15 g | ½ oz | 4 tsp baking powder
2 cl | 1 ½ tbsp coconut syrup
1 cl | ½ tbsp cherry liqueur
milk (as required)

For the frosting:
300 g | 11 oz milk chocolate
80 g | 3 oz | ⅓ cup coconut oil
100 g | 3 ½ oz | ¾ cup candied cherries
and strawberries, roughly chopped

METHOD:

Heat the oven to 180°C (160°C fan) 375°F, gas 5.

Toast the coconut flakes until golden in a dry pan.

Sprinkle with 4-6 tbsp of the sugar and stir over the heat until the coconut flakes are lightly caramelised. Set aside and leave to cool.

Cream the butter and sugar until light and fluffy then beat in the eggs.

Finely grind the caramelized coconut in a food mill or food processor.

Mix the flour with the baking powder and ground coconut flakes and stir into the egg mixture, a tablespoonful at a time, gradually adding the coconut syrup and liqueur between additions of flour. If the mixture is too stiff, add milk a tablespoonful at a time.

Spread the mixture on a 35 cm x 25 cm | 14 in x 10 in baking pan lined with baking parchment and bake for 60 minutes.

To make the frosting, put the chocolate into a bowl with the coconut oil and melt over simmering water.

Remove the cake from of the oven, lift on to a rack and remove the paper, allow to cool.

Spread thickly with the chocolate icing and scatter with candied fruit.

When the chocolate is almost set, cut the cake into 24 pieces and leave to cool completely.

BISCUITS & COOKIES.

Chocolate chip cookies

Prep and cook time: 25 minutes * Cannot be frozen * Makes: 20 - 25 cookies

INGREDIENTS:

100 g | 3 ½ oz | 1 stick softened butter
50 g | 1 ¾ oz | 1/4 cup sugar
100 g | 3 ½ oz | 1/2 cup brown sugar
1 egg
½ tsp vanilla extract
100 g | 3 ½ oz | ⅘ cup flour
75 g | 2 ½ oz | ¾ cup ground hazelnuts
1 tsp baking powder
150 g | 5 oz | ⅘ cup chocolate chips,
70% cocoa

METHOD:

Heat the oven to 200°C (180°C fan) 400°F, gas 6.

Line a cookie sheet with baking parchment.

Beat the butter, sugar and brown sugar to a creamy consistency.

Add the egg and vanilla extract and mix well.

Add the flour, hazelnuts and baking powder and quickly mix in.

Fold in the chocolate chips.

Spoon little piles of the mixture onto the baking tray, flatten slightly and bake for 10 - 15 minutes.

Remove from the baking tray and place on a cooling rack.

Frosted chocolate cookies with cream filling

Prep and cook time: 1 hour 15 minutes * Cannot be frozen * Makes: 40

INGREDIENTS:

300 g | 11 oz dark chocolate
100 g | 3 ½ oz | 1 stick butter, melted
3 eggs
250 g | 9 oz | 1 ¼ cups sugar
100 g | 3 ½ oz | ¾ cup plain|all
purpose flour
1 tsp baking powder
1 pinch salt
2 - 3 tbsp ground hazelnuts

For the filling:
200 g | 7 oz | 1 cup sour cream
100 g | 3 ½ oz | 1 cup icing|
confectioners' sugar
100 ml | 3 ½ fl oz | 7 tbsp cream
1 packet cream stabilizer

For the frosting:
250 g | 9 oz hazelnut chocolate spread
1 tbsp palm oil

METHOD:

Heat the oven to 180°C (160°C fan) 350°F, gas 3.

Melt the chocolate with the butter over simmering water.

Beat the eggs and sugar until creamy.

Mix together the flour, baking powder and salt.

Fold the dry ingredients into the chocolate butter and add the ground hazelnuts.

Place teaspoonfuls of the cookie dough on a cookie sheet and make a slight indentation in the middle of each. Bake for 8 minutes.

Remove from the oven and allow to cool on a wire rack.

Beat the sour cream until smooth with half of the icing/confectioners' sugar.

Whip the cream until stiff with 1 tsp icing/confectioners' sugar and the cream stabilizer.

Fold the whipped cream into the sour cream and sweeten with the rest of the icing/confectioners' sugar if desired.

Place a blob of cream in the centre of each cookie and chill.

Melt the hazelnut spread with the palm oil, spread thinly over the cream on each cookie and let cool.

Chocolate cream macaroons

Prep and cook time: 50 minutes * Cannot be frozen * Makes: 30

INGREDIENTS:

4 egg whites
2 tsp lemon juice
250 g | 9 oz | 1 ¼ cups caster|
superfine sugar
200 g | 7 oz | 2 cups ground almonds
2 tsp cocoa powder

For the filling:
150 g | 5 oz dark chocolate
80 ml | 3 fl oz | ⅓ cup whipping cream
20 g | ¾ oz | ¼ stick butter, chopped

To garnish:
cocoa powder to dust
paper heart stencil

METHOD:

Heat the oven to 130°C (110°C fan) 270°F, gas 1.

Beat the egg whites with the lemon juice until they form stiff peaks then gradually trickle in the sugar, still beating. Continue beating until the mixture is firm and glossy.

Carefully fold in the ground almonds.

Fold in the cocoa to lightly colour the mixture.

Spoon the mixture into a piping bag with a large round nozzle and pipe small domed circles approximately ¾" in diameter onto a cookie sheet lined with baking parchment.

Bake the macaroons for 40 minutes, leaving the oven door open a crack.

To make the filling melt the chocolate over simmering water.

Whip the cream until stiff.

Whisk the butter into the melted chocolate.

As soon as the chocolate has cooled, fold in the cream.

Sandwich the macaroons together in twos with the chocolate cream.

Put a paper stencil in the shape of a heart on top of each macaroon, dust with cocoa and carefully remove the paper stencil.

White choc chip cookies with almonds

Prep and cook time: 30 minutes ∗ Can be frozen ∗ Makes: 25

INGREDIENTS:

90 g | 3 oz | 1 stick butter, softened
150 g | 5 oz | ¼ cup brown sugar
1 egg
175 g | 6 oz | 1 ½ cups plain|
all purpose flour
½ tsp baking powder
50 g | 1 ¾ oz | ⅓ cup chopped almonds
50 g | 1 ¾ oz white chocolate chips

METHOD:

Heat the oven to 200°C (180°C fan) 400°F, gas 6 and line a cookie sheet with baking parchment.

Cream together the sugar, butter and egg.

Mix together the flour and baking powder and fold into the butter mixture along with the nuts and chocolate chips.

Using two teaspoons, spoon small piles of cookie dough onto the cookie sheet, flatten slightly and bake for 15 minutes until golden brown.

Apricot chocolate stars with glace cherries

Prep and cook time: 50 minutes * Cannot be frozen * Makes: 25 - 30

INGREDIENTS:

2 egg whites
1 pinch salt
3 tbsp icing|confectioners' sugar
500 g | 18 oz marzipan paste
4 cl | 3 tbsp apricot liqueur
2 tbsp apricot juice drink
4 egg yolks
250 g | 9 oz dark chocolate, 70% cocoa

To garnish:
glace cherries

METHOD:

Heat the oven to 200°C (180°C fan) 400°F, gas 6. Line a cookie sheet with baking parchment.

Whisk the egg whites with a pinch of salt until stiff. Add the icing/confectioners' sugar and continue whisking until glossy and forming stiff peaks.

Crumble the marzipan into small pieces and whisk using an electric whisk, adding the liqueur and apricot juice. Continue whisking and add the egg yolk little by little until smooth and creamy.

Fold in the beaten egg whites.

Spoon the mixture into a piping bag with a star nozzle and pipe small stars (3 cm high) onto the cookie sheet.

Bake for 30 minutes until golden brown. Remove from the oven and cool on a wire rack.

Halve the glace cherries and place a half on the point of each star. Allow to cool completely.

Melt the chocolate over simmering water. Dip the base of each star in the chocolate and place on baking parchment to set.

Chocolate chip cookies with rolled oats

Prep and cook time: 35 minutes * Can be frozen * Makes: 18 - 20

INGREDIENTS:

100 g | 3 ½ oz | 1 stick butter, softened
50 g | 1 ¾ oz | ¼ cup sugar
100 g | 3 ½ oz | ½ cup brown sugar
1 large egg, beaten
1 tsp vanilla extract
100 g | 3 ½ oz | ¾ cup plain|
all purpose flour
75 g | 2 ½ oz | 1 cup rolled oats
1 tsp baking powder
150 g | 5 oz | ¾ cup chocolate chips

METHOD:

Heat the oven to 180°C (160°C fan) 375°F, gas 5.

Line a cookie sheet with baking parchment.

Cream together the butter, sugar and brown sugar until light and fluffy.

Gradually add the egg and then the vanilla.

Mix the flour, rolled oats and baking powder and stir in carefully.

Fold in the chocolate chips.

Place spoonfuls of the cookie dough on the cookie sheet at 5 cm intervals and flatten slightly.

Bake for 10 to 12 minutes. Cool on the baking tray for 5 minutes. Sprinkle with toasted oats and cool thoroughly before storing.

Chocolate shortbread fingers

Prep and cook time: 45 minutes * Can be frozen * Makes: 25 – 30

INGREDIENTS:

175 g | 6 oz | 1 ½ sticks softened butter
75 g | 2 ½ oz | ½ cup icing|
confectioners' sugar
¼ tsp salt
1 vanilla pod
1 egg white
150 g | 5 oz | 1 ⅕ cup plain|
all purpose flour
50 g | 1 ¾ oz | ½ cup ground hazelnuts
25 g | 1 oz | ¼ cup cornflour|cornstarch

For decoration:
150 g | 5 oz dark chocolate

METHOD:

Heat the oven to 200°C (180°C fan) 400°F, gas 6 and line a cookie sheet with baking parchment.

Beat the butter with the icing/confectioners' sugar, salt and vanilla pod seeds and add the egg white. Beat until the mixture is light in colour.

Mix together the flour, nuts and cornflour/cornstarch and stir into the butter mixture.

Spoon the dough into a piping bag with a star nozzle.

Pipe approximately 2" long portions of dough onto a cookie sheet and bake for 12 - 15 minutes until golden. Remove from the oven and allow to cool.

To decorate, melt the chocolate over simmering water. Dip the cookies half into the chocolate, place on baking parchment and leave to set.

Chocolate madeleines

Prep and cook time: 40 minutes ∗ Cannot be frozen ∗ Makes: 4

INGREDIENTS:

100 g | 3 ½ oz |1 cup plain|
all purpose flour
100 g | 3 ½ oz dark chocolate, 70% cocoa
100 g | 3 ½ oz |½ cup butter
2 eggs
1 tsp. baking powder
120 g | 4 oz | 4 ½ oz / 1 cup
icing|confectioners' sugar
soft butter, for the madeleine moulds

METHOD:

Heat the oven to 220°C (200°C fan) 425°F, gas 5

Melt the butter. Chop the chocolate and melt in a bowl over a pan of hot water. Stir in the butter.

Beat the eggs and the sugar until light and creamy, then mix in the flour and the baking powder.

Add the chocolate and carefully stir.

Grease the madeleine moulds with butter and pour in the batter so that they are about 2/3 full.

Bake in the oven for 5 minutes. Reduce the temperature to 180°C (160°C fan) 400°F, gas 4 and bake for a further 8 - 10 minutes until ready.

Remove from the oven and allow to cool slightly, then turn out on a wire rack and cool completely.

Chocolate pecan cookies

Prep and cook time: 30 minutes ∗ Cannot be frozen ∗ Makes: 20 - 25

INGREDIENTS:

100 g | 3 ½ oz | 1 stick butter, softened
1 pinch salt
50 g | 1 ¾ oz | ¼ cup sugar
100 g | 3 ½ oz | ½ cup brown sugar
1 egg
170 g | 6 oz | 1 ½ cups plain|
all purpose flour
1 tsp baking powder
75 g | 2 ½ oz | ½ cup chocolate chips
75 g | 2 ½ oz | ⅔ cup pecan nuts,
roughly chopped

METHOD:

Heat the oven to 180°C (160°C fan) 375°F, gas 5 and line a cookie sheet with baking parchment.

Cream together the butter, salt, sugar and brown sugar, add the egg and mix well.

Mix together the flour and baking powder and carefully fold into the butter and sugar.

Melt half of the chocolate chips.

Mix the remaining chocolate chips and the pecan nuts into the cookie dough.

Place one third of the dough in a separate bowl and mix with the melted chocolate.

Return the chocolate dough to the rest of the dough and mix to achieve a marbled effect (do not mix too thoroughly or this effect will be lost).

Using a teaspoon, spoon piles of cookie dough onto the cookie sheet and bake for 12 minutes. Remove and cool on a wire rack.

Filled chocolate cookies

Prep and cook time: 45 minutes * Cannot be frozen * Makes: 40 cookies

INGREDIENTS:

200 g | 7 oz | 2 sticks butter, softened

100 g | 3 ½ oz | 1 cup icing| confectioners' sugar

3 egg yolks

1 tsp vanilla extract

1 tbsp orange juice

1 tsp cinnamon

175 g | 6 oz | 1 ⅓ cups plain| all purpose flour

75 g | 2 ½ oz | ¾ cup almonds, finely ground

2 tbsp cocoa powder

75 g | 2 ½ oz dark chocolate, 70% cocoa

40 ml | 1 ½ fl oz | 8 tsp cream

125 g | 4 ½ oz dark chocolate

METHOD:

Heat the oven to 180°C (160°C fan) 375°F, gas 5.

Cream the butter with the icing/confectioners' sugar until light and fluffy.

Beat in the egg yolks, vanilla extract, orange juice and cinnamon.

Mix the flour, ground almonds, cocoa and grated chocolate. Combine with the egg mixture and knead into a smooth dough. Wrap in cling film and chill for 30 minutes.

Roll out to a thickness of approximately ¼" on a floured work surface.

Cut out circles (4.5" in diameter) and place on a baking tray lined with baking parchment.

Bake for about 10 minutes. Remove from the baking tray with the paper and leave to cool.

Heat the cream and gradually add the rest of the dark chocolate, stirring to dissolve.

Sandwich the biscuits together in pairs with the chocolate cream. Place on a wire rack to set.

Chocolate short-crust towers with three-cream filling

Prep and cook time: 45 minutes * Chill: 1 hour * Cannot be frozen * Serves: 4

INGREDIENTS:

For the pastry:
150 g | 5 oz | 1 ¼ cups plain|
all purpose flour
60 g | 2 oz | ⅔ cup icing|
confectioners' sugar
1 good pinch ground cinnamon
2 tbsp cocoa powder
100 g | 3 ½ oz | 1 stick butter, softened

For the cream fillings:
200 ml | 7 fl oz | ⅞ cup cream
60 g | 2 oz dark chocolate,
70% cocoa, finely grated
2 cl | 4 ½ tsp rum
75 g | 2 ½ oz milk chocolate,
finely grated
2 cl | 4 ½ tsp cocoa liqueur
1 tbsp icing|confectioners' sugar

METHOD:

Heat the oven to 180°C (160°C fan) 375°F, gas 5 and line a cookie sheet with baking parchment.

Mix the flour with the icing/confectioners' sugar, cinnamon and cocoa powder. Add the butter in tiny pieces and combine with your hands to form a dough. Wrap in cling film and chill for around 30 minutes.

Roll out the dough on a floured work surface to around 3 mm thickness and cut out 20 rounds (approximately 2 ⅓"). Place on the cookie sheet and bake for about 15 minutes. Carefully remove from cookie sheet and let cool.

To make the cream fillings, heat half of the cream.

Pour half of the hot cream over the dark chocolate and add the rum. Stir until the chocolate has completely dissolved.

Pour the other half of the hot cream over the milk chocolate and add the cocoa liqueur, stirring until the chocolate has dissolved. Chill both creams for 30 minutes.

Whip the remaining cream with the icing/confectioners' sugar until stiff.

To assemble, spoon all three creams into piping bags with plain nozzles. Now alternate the chocolate rounds with the creams by alternating layers of the rounds with the different types of cream.

DESSERTS.

DESSERTS.

Chocolate sabayon

Prep and cook time: 30 minutes * Cannot be frozen * Serves: 4

INGREDIENTS:

175 ml | 6 fl oz | ¾ cup milk
80 g | 3 oz chocolate
5 egg yolks
60 g | 2 oz | ⅓ cup sugar
60 ml | 2 fl oz | ¼ cup chocolate liqueur

To garnish:
grated chocolate
raspberries

METHOD:

Put the milk into a pan and bring to a boil.

Remove the boiling milk from the heat and melt the chocolate in it.

Beat the egg yolks with the sugar and the chocolate milk over simmering water with an electric hand whisk until the mixture is thick and foamy. Remove from the heat and stir in the chocolate liqueur.

Transfer the mixture to small glasses and garnish with grated chocolate.

Chill until time to serve. Serve the glasses of chocolate sabayon on a platter with raspberries.

White chocolate tart with berries and fruit sauce

Prep and cook time: 1 hour * Cooling time: 3 hours * Cannot be frozen * Serves: 8

INGREDIENTS:

For the pastry:
200 g | 7 oz | 1 ½ cups plain/
all purpose flour
4 tbsp sugar
1 pinch salt
100 g | 3 ½ oz | 1 stick butter,
cold, chopped
1 egg
baking parchment
dried pulses for blind baking

For the filling:
300 g | 11 oz white chocolate, chopped
70 g | 1 ¾ oz | ¼ cup crème fraiche,
low-fat
100 g | 3 ½ oz | 1 stick butter, softened

To decorate:
redcurrants
raspberries
blueberries
raspberry sauce to drizzle (if desired)

METHOD:

Heat the oven to 200°C (180°C fan) 400°F, gas 6.

Put the flour in a heap on a work surface, mix with the sugar and salt and made a well in the middle. Scatter the cold butter in the well, break an egg into the middle and add about 30 ml / 1 fl oz of lukewarm water.

Cut all ingredients together with a knife until the mixture resembles breadcrumbs.

Quickly knead to form a dough with your hands, shape into a ball, wrap in cling film and allow to rest in a cool place for about 30 minutes.

Roll out the pastry on a lightly floured work surface and line the greased 23 cm | 9 in baking pan with the pastry.

Cut the baking parchment to the size of the pan, place over the pastry, weight down with the pulses and bake for about 20 minutes.

Remove the pulses and the baking paper and let the pastry cool.

To make the filling, melt the chopped chocolate over simmering water.

Heat the crème fraiche in a saucepan and stir in the melted chocolate then gradually add the softened butter.

Pour the mixture into the pastry case, spread smoothly and allow to cool for about 2 - 3 hours.

Serve with berries and raspberry sauce.

Chocolate cream layer tartlet

Prep and cook time: 50 minutes * Waiting time: 1 hour * Cannot be frozen * Serves: 4

INGREDIENTS:

200 g | 7 oz marzipan paste
120 g | 4 oz | $^3/_5$ cup sugar
1 good pinch vanilla pod
1 egg
120 ml | 4 fl oz | $^1/_2$ cup milk
70 g | 2 1/2 oz | $^1/_2$ cup plain|
all purpose flour
30 g | 1 oz | $^1/_5$ cup cocoa powder

For the filling:
300 ml | 11 fl oz | 1 $^1/_3$ cups cream
4 tbsp coffee liqueur

To garnish:
shaved chocolate curls

METHOD:

Line a cookie sheet with baking parchment and heat the oven to 200°C (180°C fan) 400°F, gas 6.

Crumble the marzipan with the sugar, the scraped seeds from the vanilla pod, egg and milk and whisk together until smooth.

Sieve the flour and cocoa powder over the bowl and fold in to the marzipan mixture.

Push the dough through a fine sieve and leave to rest for 1 hour.

Place a ring on the baking parchment, spoon in around 2 tbsp of the dough and smooth. Remove the ring and repeat until all the dough is used up.

Bake for 6 - 7 minutes and immediately remove the dough circles carefully with a palate knife, place on a work surface and let cool.

To fill, whip the cream and liqueur stiffly and layer up with the chocolate circles. End with cream as the top layer, dust with cocoa powder and serve decorated with shaved chocolate.

Profiteroles with chocolate sauce

Prep and cook time: 1 hour * Cannot be frozen * Makes: 35 - 40 profiteroles

------

INGREDIENTS:

For the chocolate sauce:
250 ml | 9 fl oz | 1 cup milk
100 ml | 3 ½ fl oz | 7 tbsp cream
100 g | 3 ½ oz dark chocolate, 70% cocoa
1 tbsp rum
1 tbsp cocoa powder
40 g | 1 ½ oz | 3 ½ tbsp sugar
1 tsp cornflour|cornstarch

For the profiteroles:
1 pinch salt
50 g | 1 ¾ oz | ½ stick butter
150 g | 5 oz | 1 cup 4 tbsp plain|
all purpose flour
1 - 2 tbsp cornflour|cornstarch
1 tsp baking powder
4 eggs

To decorate:
200 ml | 7 fl oz | ⅞ cup cream,
2 tbsp icing|confectioners' sugar

METHOD:

Heat the oven to 200°C (180°C fan) 400°F, gas 6 and line a cookie sheet with baking parchment.

To make the chocolate sauce, heat the milk and cream, add the chocolate and stir to dissolve. Stir in the rum, cocoa powder and sugar.

Mix the cornflour/cornstarch to a paste with 1 tbsp of water, stir into the sauce and heat through, do not allow the mixture to boil. Remove from the heat and allow to cool, stirring occasionally.

To make the profiteroles, pour 250ml (1 cup) of water into a pan and place all other pastry ingredients near to hand.

Briefly bring the water to a boil with the salt and butter. Mix the flour with the cornflour/cornstarch and baking powder and tip into the pan in one go, stirring vigorously all the time.

Continue stirring the dough until it forms a ball and leaves the sides of the pan clean. Continue stirring and turning the dough until a white film forms on the base of the pan.

Tip the dough into a bowl, allow to cool and then mix in the eggs one by one using the dough hook of a hand-held mixer.

Fill a piping bag with a large nozzle with the choux pastry dough and pipe around 40 walnut-sized balls onto the cookie sheet.

Bake for 12-15 minutes, remove from the oven and allow to cool.

Whip the cream and icing/confectioners' sugar until stiff and spoon into a piping bag with a small nozzle.

Cut a hole in the side of each profiterole using scissors and fill with cream.

Arrange the profiteroles on a large plate and drizzle with the chocolate sauce.

White chocolate cream with chocolate sauce and cherries

Prep and cook time: 45 minutes * Cooling time: 4 hours * Can be frozen * Serves: 4

INGREDIENTS:

For the cream:
150 ml | 5 fl oz | ⅔ cup milk
1 vanilla pod
60 g | 2 oz | ⅓ cup sugar
100 g | 3 ½ oz white chocolate
200 ml | 7 fl oz | ⅞ cup whipping cream
6 sheets gelatine, soaked in cold water
200 g | 7 oz | ¾ cup natural yoghurt

For the chocolate sauce:
125 ml | 4 ½ fl oz | ½ cup milk
100 ml | 3 ½ fl oz | 7 tbsp whipping cream
½ vanilla pod
150 g | 5 oz dark chocolate, 70 % cocoa
75 g | 2 ½ oz | ¾ stick butter, softened

a few cherries, to decorate

METHOD:

To make the cream, heat the milk in a pan with the seeds scraped out of the vanilla pod, the vanilla pod and the sugar.

Remove from the heat and melt the chocolate in the hot milk. Allow it to cool completely.

Softly whip the cream.

Squeeze any excess water from the gelatine and put into a small pan with 3 tablespoons of the chocolate milk. Heat gently over a low heat until the gelatine has dissolved.

Stir in the rest of the chocolate milk and the yoghurt and fold in the cream.

Fill individual moulds, cover and chill for 4 hours.

For the chocolate sauce put the milk and cream into a pan with the vanilla pod (slit open) and bring to a boil.

Pour onto the cooking chocolate and melt carefully.

Beat the softened butter and gradually stir the chocolate milk mixture into the butter.

To serve, briefly dip the moulds in hot water and turn out on to dessert plates. Add chocolate sauce and cherries and serve.

Chocolate cheesecake

Prep and cook time: 35 minutes * Chilling time: 4 hours * Can be frozen * Serves: 10 - 12

INGREDIENTS:

200 g | 7 oz | 1 ½ cup chocolate cookies
100 g | 3 ½ oz | 1 stick butter, melted
good pinch ground cinnamon
100 g | 3 ½ oz dark chocolate, 70% cocoa
1 tbsp coffee liqueur
100 g | 3 ½ oz white chocolate, chopped
1 vanilla pod
200 g | 7 oz | 1 cup crème fraiche
250 g | 9 oz | 1 ¼ cup mascarpone
80 g | 3 oz | 6 ½ tbsp sugar

METHOD:

Crush the chocolate cookies and mix well with the melted butter and cinnamon.

Spread onto the base of a 23 cm | 9 in spring form pan and firm down. Chill for around 30 minutes in the refrigerator.

Melt the dark chocolate over simmering water, stirring constantly and stir in the coffee liqueur.

In a separate bowl, melt the white chocolate over simmering water.

Split the vanilla pod open lengthways and scrape out the seeds.

Beat the crème fraiche, mascarpone and sugar together until smooth.

Split the mascarpone mixture into two halves. Stir the dark chocolate into one half and the white chocolate and vanilla seeds into the other half.

Spread both chocolate mixtures onto the base. Create swirling patterns by drawing a fork across the surface. Chill for at least 3 hours before serving.

Chocolate cakes with chocolate sauce

Prep and cook time: 50 minutes * Can be frozen * Makes: 10 individual cakes
---

INGREDIENTS:

For the chocolate cakes:
70 g | 2 ½ oz | ¾ cup ground walnuts
1 vanilla pod
250 ml | 9 fl oz | 1 cup milk
150 g | 5 oz dark chocolate, 70% cocoa
125 g | 4 ½ oz | 1 stick butter
125 g | 4 ½ oz | 1 cup plain|
all purpose flour
8 egg whites
8 egg yolks
100 g | 3 ½ oz | ½ cup sugar butter and
sugar for the ramekins

To decorate:
200 g | 7 oz dark chocolate, 70% cocoa

METHOD:

Heat the oven to 180°C (160°C fan) 375°F, gas 5.

Toast the walnuts in a dry skillet until fragrant. Remove and let cool.

Slit the vanilla pod lengthways and scrape out the seeds. Place the seeds and the bean pod in a pan with the milk and bring to a boil.

Melt the chocolate over simmering water.

Melt the butter in a pan, stir in the flour and cook briefly to make a roux.

Remove the vanilla pod from the milk and stir the milk into the roux. Simmer gently for 10 minutes, stirring occasionally.

Pour the mixture into a large bowl, let cool slightly and stir in 2 egg whites.

Add the egg yolks one by one, stirring the mixture to a smooth consistency each time.

Add the melted chocolate and nuts.

Beat the remaining egg whites and sugar until stiff and whisk about ¼ into the chocolate mixture. Fold the rest of the egg whites in carefully using a spatula.

Butter the ramekins and scatter with sugar. Pipe the cake batter into the ramekins using a piping bag with a large nozzle. Fill the ramekins only ¾ full (the cakes will rise in the oven).

Place the ramekins in a bain marie and bake in the oven for 35 minutes. Test with a wooden toothpick, if it comes out clean, the cake is ready.

Remove from the oven and whilst still hot, pour over melted chocolate. Leave to cool and serve.

Chocolate parfait with chilli and kumquats

Prep and cook time: 50 minutes * Freezing time: 6 hours * Can be frozen * Serves: 6

INGREDIENTS:

For the parfait:

75 g | 2 ½ oz | 6 tbsp sugar
5 egg yolks
2 tbsp cocoa powder
4 tbsp cocoa liqueur
250 ml | 9 fl oz | 1 cup whipping cream
½ tsp chilli powder nutmeg
espresso powder, for sprinkling

For the kumquats:

300 g | 11 oz kumquats
60 g | 2 oz | 5 ½ tbsp sugar
300 ml | 11 fl oz | 1 ⅓ cups orange juice
20 g | ¾ oz | 1 ½ tbsp ginger,
freshly chopped
1 tsp cornflour|cornstarch

METHOD:

Put the sugar and egg yolks into a mixing bowl with 50 ml water and beat over a pan of simmering water with an electric whisk until thick and creamy.

Mix the cocoa powder to a smooth paste with the cocoa liqueur and stir into the mixture. Remove from the heat and whisk until cold.

Whip the cream until stiff and fold in. Season with the chilli and nutmeg.

Transfer the mixture to tall, narrow moulds, cover and freeze for 6 hours.

Prick the kumquats several times with a needle and blanch in boiling water for 1 minute. Drain, refresh in cold water, drain thoroughly and halve.

Caramelize the sugar in a saucepan until light brown, then add the orange juice and ginger and boil to reduce by a third.

Mix the cornflour/cornstarch to a smooth paste with a little water and stir into the syrup. Bring to the boil and allow the mixture to thicken.

Add the kumquats, return to the boil, then remove from the heat and leave to cool.

To serve, dip the moulds quickly in hot water and turn the parfaits out of the moulds. Sprinkle with espresso powder and serve with the kumquats.

Chocolate bombe with raspberries

Prep and cook time: 1 hour * Freezing time: 2 hour 30 minutes * Cannot be frozen * Serves: 8 - 1

INGREDIENTS:

For the sponge cake:
5 eggs, separated
120 g | 4 oz icing|confectioners' sugar
50 g | 1 ¾ oz | ½ cup cornflour|cornstarch
50 g | 1 ¾ oz | ½ cup plain|
all purpose flour

For the filling:
2 cl | 4 tsp brandy
2 cl | 4 tsp almond liqueur
200 g | 7 oz dark chocolate, 70% cocoa
1000 ml | 35 fl oz | 4 cups cream
50 g | 1 ¾ oz | ¼ cup almonds, peeled,
chopped and toasted
50 g | 1 ¾ oz | ¼ cup hazelnuts (cob nuts),
peeled, chopped and toasted
50 g | 1 ¾ oz crumbled meringue
50 g | 1 ¾ oz | ½ cup icing|
confectioners' sugar

To serve:
100 g | 3 ½ oz dark chocolate, melted
400 g | 14 oz | 2 ½ cups raspberries

METHOD:

Heat the oven to 220°C (200°C fan) 425°F, gas 7.

To make the sponge, beat all of the sponge ingredients together until light and creamy. Spread the batter onto large cookie sheet and bake for 12 minutes.

Line a deep, rounded 1.2 litre | 2 pint bowl with cling film.

Cut a circle the same size as the base of the bowl out of the sponge cake and place in the bowl. Reserve around ⅓ of the sponge for the filling. Cut the remainder into strips and use to line the sides of the bowl up to the rim.

Mix together the brandy and almond liqueur and brush onto the sponge in the bowl until saturated. Place in the refrigerator.

To make the filling, coarsely grate half the chocolate. Roughly chop the remaining chocolate and place in a bowl. Bring ½ cup cream to a boil and stir into the chopped chocolate until it has completely dissolved and let cool.

Whip the remaining cream with the icing/confectioners' sugar until stiff and fold in the grated chocolate, almonds and hazelnuts.

Divide the whipped cream into two portions. Fold the crumbled meringue into half the cream. Mix the other half of the cream with the melted chocolate. Spoon the meringue cream into the bowl and spread over the sponge right up to the top. Place in the freezer for 20 minutes.

Remove and fill the bowl with the chocolate cream. Smooth the surface and cover with the remaining sponge strips. Freeze for 2 hours.

To serve, coat the bombe with the melted chocolate and return to the freezer for 10 minutes. Remove and garnish with fresh raspberries.

Chocolate-glazed pears

Prep and cook time: 30 minutes ∗ Cannot be frozen ∗ Serves: 4

INGREDIENTS:

4 large, firm pears
Juice of 1 lemon
100 g | 3 ½ oz dark chocolate
100 g | 3 ½ oz white cooking chocolate

Also:
50 ml | 1 ¾ fl oz | 10 tsp dry white wine
1 - 2 tbsp sugar
100 g | 3 ½ oz candied peel
2 tbsp butter

METHOD:

Heat the oven to 180°C (160°C fan) 375°F, gas 5.

Wash and peel the pears, but leave the stalks on. Level off the bottoms and drizzle lemon juice over the top.

Place the pears on a cookie sheet and bake in the oven for about 1 5 minutes. Remove from the oven.

Melt the cooking chocolate in separate bowls over a pan of boiling water.

Coat two pears with the dark cooking chocolate and two pears with the white cooking chocolate.

Boil the wine and sugar together with the chopped candied peel until the liquid has a syrupy consistency, adding a little butter to taste.

Arrange the pears on a plate, drizzle a little of the syrup around the pears and serve.

Chocolate espresso panna cotta

Prep and cook time: 50 minutes * Chill: 5 minutes * Cannot be frozen * Makes: 4

INGREDIENTS:

For the chocolate panna cotta:
4000 ml | 141 fl oz | 17 cups of gelatine,
soaked in cold water
150 ml | 5 fl oz | ¾ cup cream, 30% fat
150 ml | 5 fl oz | ¾ cup milk
100 ml | 3 ½ fl oz | 7 tbsp espresso
100 g | 3 ½ oz dark chocolate
(60% cocoa), chopped
2 tbsp sugar

For the espresso layer:
250 ml | 9 fl oz | 1 cup espresso
3000 ml | 106 fl oz | 13 cups of gelatine,
soaked in cold water
1 tbsp sugar

For the vanilla panna cotta:
180 ml | 6 fl oz | ¾ cup milk
3000 ml | 106 fl oz | 13 cups of gelatine,
soaked in cold water
1/2 tsp vanilla extract
1 tbsp sugar
100 ml | 3 ½ fl oz | 7 tbsp cream, 30% fat

METHOD:

To make the chocolate panna cotta, bring the cream, milk, espresso and sugar to a boil and remove from the heat.

Add the chocolate, stirring until dissolved.

Squeeze the gelatine to remove excess water and dissolve in the chocolate mixture.

Mix well and divide between 4 glasses. Chill for at least 2 hours.

To make the espresso layer, squeeze the gelatine to remove the excess water and dissolve in a pan with 3 tbsp espresso over a low heat. Stir into the espresso and sweeten with sugar.

Let cool and pour around ⅔ of the espresso mixture onto the set chocolate layer.

Chill in the refrigerator for at least 1 hour until set.

Pour the rest of the espresso mixture into a shallow dish lined with plastic wrap and chill in the refrigerator until set.

To make the vanilla panna cotta, bring the milk to a boil, stirring constantly. Add the vanilla extract, sugar and cream.

Squeeze the gelatine to remove excess water and dissolve in a pan with 3 tbsp of the vanilla milk over a low heat.

Stir into the vanilla milk and chill in the refrigerator until just beginning to set then pour onto the espresso layer.

Chill in the refrigerator for a further 2 hours until set.

To serve, turn out the reserved espresso jelly and chop into small cubes. Divide between the glasses and serve.

Chocolate crêpes

Prep and cook time: 2 hours * Cannot be frozen * Serves: 4

INGREDIENTS:

For the crêpe batter:
100 g | 3 ½ oz | ¾ cup plain|
all purpose flour
1 tbsp sugar
1 tbsp cocoa powder
1 pinch salt
2 eggs
2 egg yolks
2 tbsp melted butter
125 ml | 4 ½ fl oz | ½ cup milk
80 ml | 3 fl oz | ⅓ cup mineral
water, sparkling

For the filling:
100 g | 3 ½ oz dark chocolate
4 tbsp strong espresso
2 eggs, separated
1 tsp vanilla extract
1 tbsp sugar
100 ml | 3 ½ fl oz | 7 tbsp chilled cream
cocoa powder, for sprinkling
cinnamon sugar, for sprinkling
1 tbsp sugar
100 g | 3 ½ oz | ½ cup cream
cocoa powder, for sprinkling
cinnamon sugar, for sprinkling

METHOD:

To make the pancake batter, mix the flour, sugar, cocoa powder, salt, eggs, egg yolks and melted butter. Gradually whisk in the milk to make a smooth batter. Allow to rest for 1 hour.

Heat a large pan and add a little butter.

While the butter is melting, stir the mineral water into the pancake batter.

Add a small ladleful of mixture to the pan and tilt it so the mixture covers the pan evenly. When bubbles form on the surface, turn the pancake over and cook the other side. Take out of the pan and allow to cool.

Repeat the process until all the pancake mixture is used up.

For the filling melt the chocolate with the espresso over simmering water. Remove from the heat and leave to cool.

Beat the egg yolks with the vanilla extract and sugar over the simmering water until the sugar has dissolved and the mixture is thick and creamy.

Whip the chilled cream until stiff. Beat the egg whites with the sugar until they form stiff peaks.

Add the egg yolk mixture to the chocolate and stir in with a whisk.

Tip the whipped cream onto the chocolate mixture and quickly stir in with the whisk, before the mixture sets.

Carefully fold in the beaten egg whites.

To serve, spread a little of the chocolate cream on each crêpe, fold over or roll up and arrange on plates. Serve sprinkled with cocoa and cinnamon sugar.

Chocolate raspberry tart

Prep and cook time: 40 minutes ∗ Chill: 4 hours ∗ Cannot be frozen ∗ Serves: 8 - 10

INGREDIENTS:

Chocolate short-crust pastry:
150 g | 5 oz | 1 1/5 cups plain|
all purpose flour
100 g | 3 1/2 oz | 1 stick butter, cold
50 g | 1 3/4 oz | 1/2 cup icing|
confectioners' sugar
1 tbsp cocoa powder
1 egg yolk
1 pinch salt

To blind bake:
dried pulses

For the chocolate filling:
150 g | 5 oz dark chocolate, 70% cocoa
300 ml | 11 fl oz | 1 1/3 cups cream
2 egg yolks

Also:
500 g | 18 oz | 3 1/3 cups raspberries
icing|confectioners' sugar to dust

METHOD:

Heat the oven to 200°C (180°C fan) 400°F, gas 6.

Combine the flour, butter, icing/confectioners' sugar, cocoa powder, egg yolk and salt to make a short-crust pastry dough. Roll into a ball, cover with cling film and chill for at least 1 hour in the refrigerator.

Roll out the dough and line a 23 cm | 9 in tart pan. Trim the edges and pierce the base several times with a fork.

Cut out a round of baking parchment and lay in the pastry case. Fill with the dried pulses and blind bake for 20 minutes. Remove the paper and pulses and allow to cool.

To make the filling, bring 1/4 of the cream to a boil in a saucepan, add the chopped chocolate and melt, stirring constantly. Remove from the heat and allow to cool.

Beat the egg yolks to a creamy consistency and whip the cream until stiff.

Mix the egg yolks into the chocolate and fold in the cream.

Spread the chocolate mixture onto the cooled short-crust pastry cases.

Divide the raspberries between the cases and chill for at least 3 hours.

Dust with icing/confectioners' sugar and serve.

Chocolate hazelnut parfait with chocolate sauce

Prep and cook time: 40 minutes * Freezing time: 4 hours * Can be frozen * Serves: 4

INGREDIENTS:

1 vanilla pod
250 ml | 9 fl oz | 1 cup milk
60 g | 1 ¾ oz | ½ cup ground hazelnuts
2 egg yolks
60 g | 1 ¾ oz | ⅓ cup sugar
100 g | 3 ½ oz dark chocolate, 70% cocoa, grated
4 cl 3 tbsp rum
150 ml | 5 fl oz | ⅔ cup cream

for the chocolate sauce:
100 ml | 3 ½ fl oz | 7 tbsp cream
1 tbsp honey
150 g | 5 oz dark chocolate, 70% cocoa

to garnish:
shaved chocolate curls, 70% cocoa

METHOD:

Slit the vanilla pod open lengthways and scrape out the seeds. Place both in a pan with the milk and bring to a boil. Take out the pod and discard.

Toast the hazelnuts in a dry pan and add to the milk.

Beat the egg yolks with the sugar over simmering water. Add the milk stirring constantly until creamy but do not let the milk boil. Remove from the heat and continue beating until cold.

Stir in the grated chocolate and rum.

Whip the cream until stiff and fold into the mixture.

Spoon the mixture into moulds and freeze for at least 4 hours.

To make the chocolate sauce, heat the cream with the honey and bring briefly to a boil. Stir into the chopped chocolate until it is smooth and creamy.

To serve, plunge the moulds briefly into hot water, invert on plates and garnish with the chocolate sauce and shaved chocolate curls.

Chocolate mascarpone semifreddo with berries

Prep and cook time: 1 hour * Chill: 4 hours * Cannot be frozen * Serves: 10 - 12

INGREDIENTS:

For the base:
30 g | 1 oz | ¼ stick butter
2 eggs, separated
50 g | 1 ¾ oz | ¼ cup sugar
50 g | 1 ¾ oz | 8 tbsp plain|
all purpose flour
1 tsp baking powder
30 g | 1 oz dark chocolate, 70% cocoa

For the mascarpone semifreddo:
600 g | 21 oz | 3 cups mascarpone
150 g | 5 oz | 1 ½ cups icing|
confectioners' sugar
4 tbsp lemon zest
250 ml | 9 fl oz | 1 cup milk
120 g | 4 oz dark chocolate, 70% cocoa
200 ml | 7 fl oz | ⅞ cup cream
raspberry brandy for soaking
250 g | 9 oz | 1 ⅔ cup fresh raspberries

METHOD:

Heat the oven to 200°C (180°C fan) 400°F, gas 6.

Line the base of the spring form pan with baking parchment and lightly grease the sides. Beat the egg whites until they form stiff peaks. Beat the egg yolks and sugar in a separate bowl until pale and creamy.

Mix the flour with the baking powder, sieve it on to the egg yolk mixture and pour in the butter (don't stir yet!). Add one third of the beaten egg white and stir in with the butter and the flour.

Melt the chocolate over simmering water and stir into the mixture. Carefully fold in the rest of the beaten egg white.

Transfer the mixture to a 23 cm | 9 in spring form pan and bake for 20 - 30 minutes. Release the cake from the spring form pan and turn out on to a wire rack.

To make the mascarpone semifreddo, mix the mascarpone and icing/confectioners' sugar and stir in the lemon zest and milk.Whip the cream until stiff and fold into the mascarpone with a whisk. Divide the mixture in two portions, melt the chocolate and stir in one portion.

Turn both mixtures into separate shallow containers and freeze, stirring well every 20 - 30 minutes until the mixtures have a thick, creamy consistency. The ice creams should be semi-frozen, but should still be very creamy.

Place the sponge base on a cake plate or a large plate and sprinkle with 3 - 4 tbsp raspberry brandy. Top with the chocolate ice cream. Then top with 100 g raspberries. Add the white partly frozen mascarpone ice cream and smooth the top. Put the whole cake back into the freezer for 2 hours.

To serve, garnish with the remaining raspberries.

Chocolate pudding with vanilla ice cream

Prep and cook time: 40 minutes * Cannot be frozen * Serves: 4

INGREDIENTS:

For the pudding:
150 g | 5 oz dark chocolate
100 g | 3 ½ oz | 1 stick butter
2 eggs
2 egg yolks
60 g | 2 oz | ⅓ cup sugar
2 tbsp plain|all purpose flour

To garnish:
40 g | 1 ½ oz dark chocolate
1 tbsp butter
4 scoops vanilla ice cream

METHOD:

Heat the oven to 175°C (155°C fan) 350°F, gas 4.

Melt the chocolate with the butter over a low heat.

Whisk the eggs, egg yolks and sugar with an electric whisk.

Stir in the flour and the chocolate-butter mixture.

Grease 4 ramekins and sprinkle with sugar. Fill ¾ full with the mixture and bake for 15 - 20 minutes.

Make the sauce by heating the chocolate over simmering water and stirring in the butter.

Remove the chocolate puddings from the oven, add a scoop of ice cream to each ramekin, add a little of the chocolate sauce and serve immediately.

Chocolate raspberry shells

rep and cook time: 1 hour 10 minutes * Cannot be frozen * Makes: 4

INGREDIENTS:

square chocolate shells

50 g | 5 oz | 1 cup raspberries

tsp vanilla extract

) g | 3 oz dark chocolate

cl | 2 tsp raspberry brandy

good pinch cinnamon

egg yolk

) - 50 g | 1 - 1 ¾ oz | 2 - 3 tbsp sugar

tbsp whipped cream

METHOD:

Puree half of the raspberries and push through a sieve to remove the seeds.

Mix the raspberry puree with the vanilla extract.

Melt the chocolate over simmering water. Stir in the raspberry brandy and cinnamon.

Beat the egg yolk with the sugar until creamy.

Fold the melted chocolate into the egg and sugar.

Fold the whipped cream into the chocolate mixture.

Spoon half of the mixture into the chocolate cases, spread a little of the raspberry puree on top and carefully cover with the rest of the chocolate filling.

Place into the refrigerator to set for 30 - 40 minutes.

Serve garnished with the rest of the raspberries.

Chocolate mousse

Prep and cook time: 35 minutes ∗ Chill: 3 hours ∗ Cannot be frozen ∗ Serves: 4

INGREDIENTS:

150 g | 5 oz dark chocolate, 70% cocoa
20 ml | ³/₄ fl oz | 4 tsp | 1 ¹/₂ tbsp
espresso coffee
2 cl | 1 ¹/₂ tbsp cognac
2 eggs, separated
40 g | 1 ¹/₂ oz | 3 heaped tbsp sugar
75 ml | 2 ¹/₂ fl oz | ¹/₃ cup cream

To garnish:
shaved chocolate curls, 70% cocoa

METHOD:

Melt the chocolate with the cognac and espresso over simmering water and remove from the heat.

Beat the egg yolks with half the sugar until the sugar has dissolved and the mixture is pale and creamy.

Whip the chilled cream until stiff.

Beat the egg whites with the remaining sugar until they form stiff peaks.

Pour the egg yolks into the cooled chocolate and whisk to combine.

Pour the whipped cream onto the chocolate and quickly whisk to combine before the mixture sets.

Carefully fold in the beaten egg whites.

Divide the mixture between glasses and chill in the refrigerator for at least 3 hours.

Sprinkle with shaved chocolate to serve.

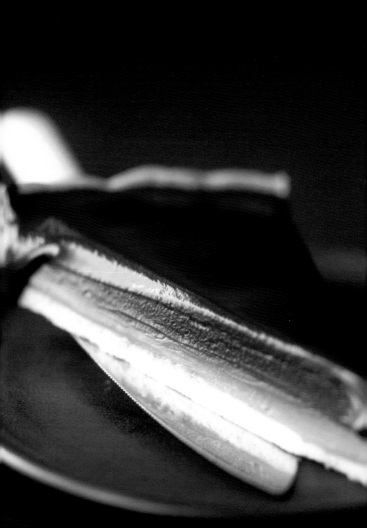

Chocolate caramel tart

Prep and cook time: 1 hour * Chill: 3 hours * Cannot be frozen * Serves: 8 - 10

INGREDIENTS:

For the pastry:
150 g | 5 oz | 1 ¼ cups plain|
all purpose flour
1 tbsp sugar
1 pinch salt
100 g | 3 ½ oz | 1 stick butter
1 egg
dried pulses to blind bake

For the light caramel layer:
400 ml | 14 fl oz | 1 ⅔ cups cream
50 g | 1 ¾ oz | ½ stick butter
200 g | 7 oz | 1 cup sugar
50 ml | 1 ¾ fl oz | 10 tsp whisky
cream liqueur

For the dark caramel layer:
300 ml | 11 fl oz | 1 ⅓ cups cream
2 tbsp sugar
1 pinch salt
120 g | 4 oz | 1 stick butter, softened
450 g | 16 oz dark chocolate
100 ml | 3 ½ fl oz | 7 tbsp milk

METHOD:

Heat the oven to 220°C (200°C fan) 425°C, gas 7.

Mix together the flour, sugar, salt, butter and eggs to make a short-crust pastry. Wrap in cling film and chill for 1 hour.

Roll the pastry out and line the 23 cm | 9 in tart pan. Trim the edges and pierce the base several times with a fork.

Cut out a round of baking parchment and lay in the pastry case. Fill with the dried pulses and blind bake for 20 minutes. Remove the paper and pulses and let cool.

To make the light caramel layer, gently simmer the cream, sugar, butter and liqueur in a pan for around 30 minutes, stirring constantly. The mixture should reduce to approximately ⅓ of the original volume and be thick and golden.

Remove the caramel from the heat and let cool slightly. Pour onto the cold pastry base and spread smooth.

To make the second caramel layer pour the cream, sugar and a pinch of salt into a pan and bring to a boil.

Remove from the heat and add the butter and chopped chocolate and stir until the chocolate has completely dissolved.

Let the mixture cool slightly. Stir in the milk until the mixture is smooth and glossy. If the mixture appears to be curdling, let it cool a little and stir in additional milk until smooth again.

Carefully spread onto the light caramel layer using a spatula. The two layers should not mix. Tip the cake gently to distribute the filling evenly and allow to cool for 1 - 2 hours before serving.

Chocolate cappuccino

Prep and cook time: 30 minutes * Chill: 2 hours * Cannot be frozen * Serves: 4

INGREDIENTS:

12 g | $^1/_2$ oz cherries, de-stoned
and quartered
100 g | 3 $^1/_2$ oz dark chocolate
40 ml | 1 $^1/_2$ fl oz | 8 tsp espresso
1 egg
2 tbsp sugar
50 ml | 1 $^3/_4$ fl oz | 10 tsp cream
1 tbsp hazelnut or peanut brittle

To garnish:
4 tbsp whipped cream
ground cinnamon to dust

METHOD:

Melt the chocolate over simmering water.

Pour the espresso into a metal bowl with the egg and sugar and beat
to a creamy consistency over simmering water.

Fold the chocolate into the egg mixture and beat until cold.

Whip the cream until stiff and fold into the mixture.

Fold in the cherries and hazelnut or peanut brittle.

Divide between 4 espresso cups and chill for at least 2 hours.

To serve, top each cappuccino with whipped cream and dust with
ground cinnamon.

Chocolate cups with white chocolate mousse

Prep and cook time: 50 minutes * Chill: 3 hours * Cannot be frozen * Serves: 4

INGREDIENTS:

For the chocolate cups:
200 g | 7 oz dark chocolate

For the mousse:
250 g | 9 oz white chocolate
4 sheets white gelatine, soaked
in cold water
4 tbsp white rum
300 ml | 11 fl oz | 1 1/3 cups whipping cream

To garnish:
30 g | 1 oz dark chocolate
100 g | 3 1/2 oz | 2/3 cup fresh raspberries
cocoa powder

METHOD:

To make the chocolate cups, cover the outside of 4 individual pudding bowls or plastic moulds with cling film.

Melt the chocolate over simmering water and coat the cling film with chocolate using a brush. Place the moulds upside down in the refrigerator and apply two more coats of chocolate, to produce a thick layer.

To make the mousse, break up the white chocolate and melt slowly over simmering water.

Squeeze out the gelatine to remove excess water, add to the chocolate and allow to dissolve. Add the rum and put into the refrigerator until it begins to set.

Whip the cream until stiff and fold into the chocolate cream.

Carefully remove the moulds from inside the chocolate cups and pull off the cling film.

Place the chocolate cups on plates, fill with chocolate mousse and chill.

Warm the rest of the chocolate, put into a small cone of parchment paper, cut off a corner and pipe a spiral on top of each chocolate mousse.

Decorate with raspberries and dust with cocoa powder.

Iced chocolate torte

Prep and cook time: 35 minutes * Freezing time: 4 hours * Can be frozen * Makes: 4

INGREDIENTS:

80 g | 3 oz dark chocolate, 70% cocoa
2 tbsp heavy cream
6 cl | 4 ½ tbsp cream sherry
50 g | 1 ¾ oz | ½ cup ground almonds
40 g | 1 ½ oz | ⅕ cup sugar
150 ml | 5 fl oz | ⅔ cup whipping cream
cocoa powder to dust

METHOD:

Set four cooking rings (8 cm diameter and 7 cm height) on a smooth base lined with baking parchment and line the rim of the rings with baking parchment.

Melt the chocolate over simmering water. Remove from the heat and stir in the heavy cream, sherry and almonds and allow to cool.

Whip the cream until stiff.

Beat the egg whites to the stiff peak stage adding the sugar little by little until glossy and firm.

Fold the cream and then the egg whites into the cooled chocolate mixture.

Spoon ¾ of the chocolate mixture into the rings and the rest into a piping bag with a star nozzle and place both into the freezer for around 2 hours.

As soon as the mixture in the rings has begun to freeze, pipe the rest of the chocolate mixture on top in a decorative pattern. Freeze for at least a further two hours.

Shortly before serving, remove from the rings, peel off the paper and dust thickly with cocoa powder.

Chocolate mousse torte with strawberries

Prep and cook time: 40 minutes * Chill: 5 hours * Cannot be frozen * Serves: 4

INGREDIENTS:

For the base:
150 g | 5 oz sponge fingers
100 g | 3 ½ oz amaretti cookies, or other almond cookies
140 g | 4 ½ oz 1 ½ sticks melted butter

For the filling:
450 g | 16 oz dark chocolate, 70% cocoa
6 leaves of gelatine, softened in cold water and drained
200 g | 7 oz 1 cup cream cheese
500 ml | 18 fl oz | 2 cups cream
5 cl | 3 tbsp almond liqueur

For garnish:
200 g | 7 oz 1 ⅓ cups strawberries, washed and sliced
100 ml | 3 ½ fl oz | 7 tbsp
whipping cream
amaretti cookies
cocoa powder to dust

METHOD:

Crush the sponge fingers and amaretti cookies with a rolling pin and mix with the melted butter. Spread on the base of a 25 cm | 10 in spring form tin using your hands, press down well and chill.

Melt the chocolate over simmering water, add the drained gelatine and dissolve in the chocolate. Allow to cool slightly, stirring constantly.

Stir in the cream cheese and almond liqueur, mix to a smooth consistency and let cool.

Whip the cream until stiff then fold into the chocolate mixture.

Spread the chocolate cream onto the torte base and smooth the surface. Chill in the refrigerator for at least 4 hours or overnight if possible.

Whip the cream softly and decorate the cake with cream and strawberry slices. Dust with cocoa powder to serve.

CUPCAKES
& MUFFINS.

Chocolate and coconut cupcakes

Prep and cook time: 1 hour * Chill: 2 hours * Cannot be frozen * Makes: 12

INGREDIENTS:

200 g | 7 oz | 1 cup mascarpone
1 tbs vanilla extract
150 g | 5 oz | ¾ cup sugar
200 g | 7 oz dark chocolate, 70% cocoa
3 eggs, separated
1 pinch salt
1 tbsp instant coffee
100 g | 3 ½ oz | ¾ cup
plain| all purpose flour
50 g | 1 ¾ oz | ½ cup cornflour|cornstarch
2 tsp baking powder
50 g | 1 ¾ oz | ½ cup shredded,
dried coconut

For the frosting:
100 ml | 3 ½ fl oz | 7 tbsp whipping cream
50 g | 1 ¾ oz white
chocolate, chopped

METHOD:

Heat the oven to 200°C (180°C fan) 400°F, gas 6.

Heat the cream, add the white chocolate, stir until melted and allow to cool.

Beat the mascarpone, vanilla extract and half of the sugar until smooth and chill.

Melt the dark chocolate over simmering water, remove from the heat and allow to cool.

Beat the egg whites with a pinch of salt until stiff.

Beat the egg yolks with the remaining sugar until thick and creamy.

Sieve the instant coffee, flour, cornflour/cornstarch and baking powder onto the egg yolks and fold in thoroughly using a spatula.

Stir the melted chocolate into the mascarpone, pour the mascarpone mixture onto the batter and mix thoroughly.

Fold the beaten egg whites into the batter.

Spoon the batter into 12 paper cake cups, stand on a cookie sheet and bake for 20 - 25 minutes.

Remove from the oven and allow to cool completely.

Toast the shredded coconut in a dry pan and allow to cool.

Remove the white frosting from the refrigerator and beat until creamy.

Spoon the frosting into a piping bag, pipe onto the cupcakes and scatter with shredded coconut.

Chocolate and coffee liqueur muffins

Prep and cook time: 45 minutes * Cooling time: 1 hour 30 minutes * Cannot be frozen * Makes: 1.

INGREDIENTS:

2 eggs
120 ml | 4 fl oz | 1/2 cup vegetable oil
100 g | 3 1/2 oz | 1/2 cup sugar
200 g | 7 oz | 1 1/2 cups plain|
all purpose flour
15 g | 1/2 oz | 4 tsp baking powder
1 pinch salt
4 tbsp coffee liqueur
2 - 3 tbsp milk, as required
100 g | 3 1/2 oz dark chocolate
50 ml | 1 3/4 fl oz | 10 tsp cream
1 tsp butter

METHOD:

Heat the oven to 220°C (200°C fan) 425°F, gas 7.

Place the paper cups in the muffin pan.

Beat the eggs and oil in a bowl, adding the sugar little by little until the mixture is thick and creamy.

In another bowl, mix together the flour, baking powder and salt and then stir into the eggs and sugar along with 3 tbsp of coffee liqueur. Add just enough milk to create a thick batter.

Spoon the batter into the muffin pan and bake in the middle of the oven for 25 minutes. Remove from the oven and allow to cool. After 5 minutes, turn out of the pan and cool completely on a wire rack.

While the muffins are baking, heat the chocolate and cream carefully in a pan, stirring constantly until the chocolate has melted. Stir in the remaining coffee liqueur and add the butter in small pieces.

Spoon the frosting onto the muffins and leave to set.

Choc-cherry mini muffins

Prep and cook time: 35 minutes * Can be frozen * Makes: 24 muffins

INGREDIENTS:

200 g | 7 oz | ⁴/₅ cup plain|
all purpose flour
1 tbsp cocoa powder
2 tsp baking powder
½ tsp baking soda
100 g | 3 ½ oz | 1 cup dried cherries,
roughly chopped
1 egg
75 g | 2 ½ oz | ⅔ cup sugar
50 ml | 1 ¾ fl oz | 10 tsp vegetable oil
250 g | 9 oz | 1 cup yoghurt
24 cherries with stalks, washed and dried

Also:
1 mini muffin pan with 24 cups
24 small paper cases

METHOD:

Heat the oven to 200°C (180°C fan) 400°F, gas 6.

Place the paper cases in the muffin pan.

In a large bowl, mix together the flour, cocoa powder, baking powder, baking soda and dried cherries.

In another bowl, beat together the egg, sugar, oil and yoghurt.

Pour the egg mixture onto the flour mixture. Mix until all ingredients are just combined and spoon the mixture into the paper cases.

Carefully slit the cherries open on the undersides and remove the stones. The stalks should remain intact.

Press one cherry into each muffin and bake for 20 minutes.

Remove from oven and leave for 5 minutes. Remove from the muffin pan and let them cool completely.

Chocolate apple bakewells

Prep and cook time: 1 hour * Chill: 1 hour * Cannot be frozen * Makes: 12

INGREDIENTS:

For the pastry:
125 g | 4 ½ oz | 1 ¼ sticks softened butter
75 g | 2 ½ oz | 6 tbsp sugar
25 g | 1 oz | ¼ cup coarsely ground hazelnuts
1 egg
1 pinch salt
200 g | 7 oz | 1 ½ cups plain|
all purpose flour
10 g | ¼ oz | 1 ½ tbsp cocoa powder
butter to grease the cake rings

For the apple compote:
100 g | 3 ½ oz | ½ cup sugar
5 medium apples, peeled, cored and
finely chopped
50 g | 1 ¾ oz | ½ stick butter

For the bakewell topping:
90 g | 3 oz | 1 stick butter, melted
90 g | 3 oz | ½ cup sugar
1 egg
20 g | ¾ oz | 4 tbsp ground almonds
20 g | ¾ oz | 4 tbsp flour

Also:
icing|confectioners' sugar to dust

METHOD:

Heat the oven to 200°C (180°C fan) 400°F, gas 6.

To make the pastry, cream together the butter and sugar and stir in the nuts, egg and salt. Add the flour and cocoa powder and combine into a smooth dough. Cover and chill in the refrigerator for 1 hour.

To make the apple compote, lightly caramelise the sugar in a heavy saucepan, add the apples and mix well. Add the butter and heat through. After a few minutes, remove from the heat and allow to cool.

To make the bakewell topping, mix the melted butter with the sugar, egg, almonds and flour.

Roll out the dough to 3 mm thickness and cut out 12 rounds for the bases of the pies. Cut out 12 strips to fit the height and circumference of the cake rings.

Grease the 12 deep 7 cm | 3 in cake rings, line with pastry and press to seal to the pastry bases.

Fill the pastry cases with compote to 1 cm below the rims and top up with the bakewell mixture. Bake for 30 - 35 minutes.

Remove from the oven, let cool for a few minutes then remove the rings. Allow to cool completely and serve dusted with icing/confectioners' sugar.

Chocolate Christmas muffins

Prep and cook time: 1 hour 20 minutes * Cannot be frozen * Makes: 45

INGREDIENTS:

150 g | 5 oz | ½ cup honey
100 g | 3 ½ oz | ½ cup brown sugar
90 g | 2 ½ oz | ¾ stick butter
or margarine
4 tbsp milk, low-fat
250 g | 9 oz | 2 cups plain|
all purpose flour
2 tsp baking powder
1 pinch cardamom
½ tsp ground cloves
1 level tsp cinnamon
1 tsp gingerbread spice
4 tbsp cocoa powder
3 eggs
100 g | 3 ½ oz | ½ cup chopped almonds

To decorate:
200 g | 7 oz marzipan
dark red food colouring
green food colouring
1 egg white
220 g | 8 oz | 2 cups icing|
confectioners' sugar

Also:
45 paper cases (gold foil)
for mini-muffins
1 mini-muffin pan

METHOD:

Heat the oven to 175°C (150°C fan) 350°F, gas 4.

Line the cups of a muffin pan with the paper cases.

Warm the honey, sugar, butter and milk until the sugar dissolves and let cool.

Sieve the flour and baking powder together. Add the spices and cocoa.

Stir the dry mixture into the cooled honey mixture. Stir in the eggs and fold in the chopped almonds.

Spoon the muffin batter into the cases. The cases should only be ⅔ full.

Bake the muffins for 25 minutes. Leave to cool slightly then take out of the tin.

To decorate, take about 50 g of the marzipan and knead in some of the dark red food colouring. Make 45 little berries.

Knead green food colouring into the rest of the marzipan. Roll the green marzipan out thinly on a little icing/confectioners' sugar, cut out 45 holly leaves and mark the veins.

Beat the egg white until stiff, trickle in the icing sugar and continue beating until the mixture is thick enough to pipe. Put into a piping bag with a rosette nozzle and pipe a rosette on each muffin.

Decorate the muffins with leaves and berries.

Orange and chocolate chip muffins

Prep and cook time: 40 minutes * Can be frozen * Makes: 12 muffins

INGREDIENTS:

300 g | 11 oz | 2 1/2 cups plain|
all purpose flour
2 1/2 tbsp baking powder
1/2 tbsp baking soda
75 g | 2 1/2 oz | 1/2 cup candied orange
peel, chopped
100 g | 3 1/2 oz | 1/2 cup caster|
superfine sugar
70 g | 2 1/2 oz | 1/3 cup chocolate chips
100 ml | 3 1/2 fl oz | 7 tbsp vegetable oil
100 ml | 3 1/2 fl oz | 7 tbsp orange juice
200 ml | 7 fl oz | 7/8 cup buttermilk
2 eggs
3 orange thin orange slices, quartered

METHOD:

Heat the oven to 180°C (160°C fan) 350°F, gas 4.

Line a muffin tin with 12 paper muffin cases.

Sieve the flour, baking powder and baking soda into a bowl. Add the orange peel, sugar and half the chocolate chips.

Pour the oil into a jug, add the orange juice, buttermilk and eggs and mix together with a fork.

Pour the wet ingredients into the dry and gently stir together until just combined.

Spoon the batter into the paper muffin cups.

Sprinkle over the rest of the chocolate chips and top each muffin with an orange quarter slice.

Bake for 25 minutes until the muffins are risen and firm.

Frosted chocolate cupcakes

Prep and cook time: 45 minutes * Cannot be frozen * Makes: 12

INGREDIENTS:

150 g | 5 oz | 1 ½ sticks butter
100 g | 3 ½ oz | ½ cup sugar
2 eggs
1 tsp vanilla extract
200 g | 7 oz | 1 ½ cups plain|
all purpose flour
1 tsp baking powder
25 g | 1 oz | 2 tbsp cocoa powder
2 tbsp milk

To decorate:
1 small egg white
200 g | 7 oz | 2 cups icing|
confectioners' sugar
12 small milk chocolates

METHOD:

Heat the oven to 180°C (160°C fan) 350°F, gas 5.

Line a muffin tin with 12 paper cases.

Cream the butter until light and fluffy, then one after the other beat in the sugar, eggs and vanilla extract.

Mix the flour, baking powder and cocoa and add to the creamed mixture with the milk, alternating additions of dry ingredients and milk.

Spoon the batter into the prepared paper cases and bake for 30 minutes. Take out of the oven, leave to cool slightly in the pan, then take out and allow to cool on a wire rack.

To decorate, beat the egg white until forming soft peaks then mix with the icing/confectioners' sugar to make a smooth, thick frosting. Put a little of the frosting on each cupcake, decorate with a chocolate and leave to set before serving.

Chocolate cheesecake muffins

Prep and cook time: 45 minutes * Can be frozen * Makes: 12 muffins

INGREDIENTS:

120 g | 4 oz | 1 stick butter
250 g | 9 oz | 1 1/4 cups sugar
4 eggs
1 kg | 35 oz | 4 1/3 cups quark
(low-fat soft cheese), well drained
40 g | 1 1/2 oz | 1/2 cup
cornflour|cornstarch
1 tsp vanilla extract
1 tsp baking powder
1 good pinch lemon zest, finely grated
1 pinch salt
125 g | 4 1/2 oz dark chocolate, 70% cocoa
icing|confectioners' sugar, to dust

METHOD:

Heat the oven to 200°C (180°C fan) 400°F, gas 6.

Grease the cups of the muffin tin with butter.

Cream together the butter and sugar and beat in the eggs one by one.

Stir in the quark, cornflour/cornstarch, vanilla extract, baking powder, lemon zest and salt.

Spoon the batter into the muffin tin and bake for 30 minutes until golden brown.

Remove from the oven, allow to cool for a few minutes then remove from the pan and cool on a wire rack.

Melt the chocolate and drizzle over the muffins. Serve dusted with icing/confectioners' sugar.

Chocolate muffins with chocolate sauce

Prep and cook time: 50 minutes * Cannot be frozen * Makes: 12 muffins

INGREDIENTS:

For the dough:

400 g | 1 ⅔ cups prunes, pitted, chopped
50 ml | 10 tsp apple juice
1 egg
80 g | ⅓ cup sugar
80 ml | ⅓ cup vegetable oil
250 ml | 1 cup natural yoghurt
250 g | 2 cups plain|all purpose flour
2 tsp baking powder
½ tsp baking soda
1 pinch salt
2 tbsp cocoa powder

To decorate:

125 g | ⅓ cup dark chocolate cake topping, ready made
50 g | ⅓ cup milk chocolate

METHOD:

Heat the oven to 180°C (160°C fan) 375°F, gas 5.

Place 12 paper baking cups in the muffin pan. Knead the prunes in the apple juice by hand until the prunes have absorbed the juice.

Beat the egg with the sugar, oil and yoghurt. In another bowl, mix the flour with the baking powder, baking soda, salt and cocoa powder. Mix the egg mixture into the flour and beat quickly until all the dry ingredients are moist.

Spoon half the dough into the paper cups. Spoon over a little prune mixture and top with the remaining dough.

Bake on the middle shelf for 20 - 25 minutes. Test with a wooden toothpick, if it comes out clean the muffins are done. Cool on a wire rack.

To decorate, prepare the chocolate topping as instructed on the packet. Pour over the muffins. Scrape the milk chocolate with a potato peeler or the back of a knife to make scrolls or shavings and sprinkle them over the topping before it dries.

Chocolate cherry muffins

Prep and cook time: 30 minutes ∗ Can be frozen ∗ Makes: 12 muffins

INGREDIENTS:

100 g | 3 ½ oz butter
100 g | 3 ½ oz dark chocolate
225 g | 8 oz | 2 ¼ cup plain|
all purpose flour
150 g | 5 oz caster|superfine sugar
1 tbsp baking powder
¼ tsp baking (bicarbonate) of soda
1 egg, beaten
250 ml | 9 fl oz | 1 cup vanilla yoghurt
1 tbs vanilla extract
18 glace cherries, halved
icing|confectioners' sugar, sieved

METHOD:

Heat the oven to 190°C (170°C fan) 375°F, gas 5. Line a muffin tray with paper muffin cases.

Divide the butter into 2 bowls. Melt the butter gently over simmering water.

Break up the chocolate and add to the other bowl of butter. Melt over simmering water, stirring gently.

Sieve the flour into a bowl and add the sugar, baking powder and bicarbonate of soda.

In a jug, mix the egg, yoghurt and vanilla.

Pour the wet ingredients into the bowl, along with the melted butter and stir gently together.

Spoon ⅔ of the mixture into the melted butter and chocolate and mix together.

Put a spoonful of chocolate mix in the base of each muffin case.

Spoon on all the vanilla mixture, dividing equally between the 12.

Top with the rest of the chocolate mixture.

Arrange glace cherry halves in the top of each one.

Bake for 20 minutes until the muffins are firm and well risen. Insert a toothpick into the centre of one of the muffins, if it comes out clean, the muffins are ready.

Serve dusted with icing/confectioners' sugar.

Chocolate banana muffins

Prep and cook time: 35 minutes * Chill: 2 hours * Cannot be frozen * Makes: 20 muffins

INGREDIENTS:

100 g | 3 ½ oz dark chocolate
100 g | 3 ½ oz | 1 stick butter
4 eggs
150 g | 5 oz | ¾ cup sugar
70 g | 2 oz | ½ cup plain|
all purpose flour

2 tbsp cocoa powder
1 banana, peeled and sliced
2 tbsp brown sugar

METHOD:

Heat the oven to 200°C (180°C fan) 400°F, gas 6.

Melt the chocolate over simmering water, stirring in the butter in small pieces. Do not allow the chocolate to get too hot.

Beat the eggs and sugar until creamy and fold in the melted chocolate.

Sieve the flour and cocoa powder onto the egg mixture and fold in.

Cover the batter and chill for 2 hours.

Grease the muffin pan and dust with flour.

Spoon the batter into the pan cups (or use a piping bag if you find it easier) and place a slice of banana on top of each.

Bake for 20 minutes. Remove from the oven and allow to cool slightly. Remove from the muffin pan, sprinkle with brown sugar and leave to cool completely.

Mini chocolate cakes with cream

Prep and cook time: 50 minutes * Cannot be frozen * Makes: 12

INGREDIENTS:

For the batter:
150 g | 5 oz chocolate, 70% cocoa
150 g | 5 oz | 1 ½ sticks softened butter
100 g | 3 ½ oz | 1 cup icing|confectioners'
sugar
6 eggs, separated
75 g | 2 ½ oz | 6 tbsp sugar
125 g | 4 ½ oz | 1 cup plain|
all purpose flour
50 g | 1 ¾ oz | ½ cup ground walnuts

For the filling:
75 g | 2 ½ oz | ¼ cup apricot
jelly, warmed

For the frosting:
250 g | 9 oz dark chocolate, 70% cocoa
150 g | 5 oz milk chocolate

For decoration:
100 ml | 3 ½ fl oz | 7 tbsp cream
fruit of your choice, e. g. banana,
candied cherries

METHOD:

Heat the oven to 180°C (160°C fan) 375°F, gas 5.

Grease the 12 large muffin pans and dust with flour.

To make the cake batter, melt the chocolate over simmering water.

Cream together the butter and icing/confectioners' sugar and stir in the egg yolks and chocolate little by little.

Beat the egg whites and sugar until stiff and fold carefully into the chocolate mixture.

Mix together the flour and walnuts and fold into the mixture.

Spoon the batter into the muffin pans and bake for 30 minutes.

Remove from the oven, allow to cool for a few minutes then turn out of the pans and allow to cool completely.

Neatly slice off the tops to give a flat surface and chop the removed cake tops finely in a food processor.

Slice each cake through the middle horizontally, spread with the warm jelly and place the two parts together.

To make the frosting, melt the chocolate over simmering water and allow to cool.

Coat the cakes completely with the chocolate, cover the sides in the cake crumbs and leave to set.

Whip the cream until stiff and decorate the cakes with cream and fruit.

FANCIES.

Chocolate tartlets with fresh strawberries

Prep and cook time: 45 minutes * Chill: 1 hour * Cannot be frozen * Serves: 4

INGREDIENTS:

For the pastry:
125 g | 4 ½ oz | 1 cup plain|
all purpose flour
1 pinch salt
30 g | 1 oz | 2 ½ tbsp sugar
50 g | 1 ¾ oz | ½ stick butter, cold,
chopped into small pieces
1 egg

For the mousse:
150 g | 5 oz dark chocolate, 70% cocoa
50 ml | 1 ¾ fl oz | 10 tsp | 3 tbsp espresso
2 egg yolks
30 g | 1 oz | 2 ½ tbsp sugar
100 ml | 3 ½ fl oz | 7 tbsp cream

To garnish:
250 g | 9 oz | 1 ½ cups strawberries
chocolate curls

METHOD:

Heat the oven to 180°C (160°C fan) 375°F, gas 5.

To make the pastry, pour the flour onto a work surface in a heap, mix in the salt and sugar and make a hollow in the centre of the heap. Distribute the butter pieces around the hollow and crack the egg in the centre.

Cut all ingredients in using a knife until the mixture resembles breadcrumbs. Knead to form a dough, roll into a ball, wrap in cling film and chill for 30 minutes.

Melt the chocolate with the espresso over simmering water. Remove from the heat and let cool.

Beat the egg yolks and sugar until thick and creamy and all the sugar has dissolved. Whip the chilled cream until stiff.

Fold the chocolate into the egg yolk mixture. Pour the whipped cream onto the chocolate and quickly but carefully whisk to combine.

Spoon the mixture into a piping bag with a large nozzle and place in the refrigerator to chill for around 30 minutes until beginning to firm.

Roll the pastry dough out on a floured work surface to about 4 mm thick. Cut out 8 rounds of 4" diameter, place on a cookie sheet lined with baking parchment and bake for 10-12 minutes until golden brown. Remove and allow to cool.

Chop the strawberries into slices and some into halves.

To serve, pipe half of the mousse onto the middle of 4 pastry rounds and top with the remaining 4 rounds. Pipe the remaining mousse onto the top of the upper pastry rounds. Decorate the sides with the sliced strawberries and garnish the tops with halved strawberries and chocolate curls. Serve well chilled.

Truffle mousse meringues

Prep and cook time: 35 minutes * Cannot be frozen * Makes: 30 - 35

INGREDIENTS:

5 egg whites
200 g | 7 oz | 2 cups icing|
confectioners' sugar
2 tbsp cocoa powder
1 pinch salt

For the filling:
100 ml | 3 ½ fl oz | 7 tbsp cream
200 g | 7 oz white chocolate

To garnish:
cocoa powder to dust

METHOD:

Heat the oven to 120°C (100°C fan) 225°F, gas 3.

Mix together the egg whites, icing/confectioners' sugar, cocoa powder and salt.

Beat the egg white mixture over simmering water until it is creamy and has reached a temperature of 50°C (120°F). Remove from the simmering water and slowly beat until cold.

Spoon the mixture into a piping bag with nozzle and pipe walnut-sized heaps onto a cookie sheet lined with baking parchment.

Place in the oven for 2 hours to dry out. Remove and allow to cool.

To make the filling, melt the white chocolate with the cream over simmering water, allow to cool and then beat with an electric whisk until creamy.

Spoon the cream into a piping bag with a star nozzle and pipe a little onto half of the meringues, top with the remaining halves, press to firm and serve dusted with cocoa powder.

Chocolate apples with nuts

Prep and cook time: 20 minutes * Cannot be frozen * Makes: 6

INGREDIENTS:

125 g | 4 ½ oz | ¾ cup hazelnuts
(cog nuts), roughly chopped
6 small unblemished apples, washed
and dried
180 g | 6 oz white chocolate, chopped
180 g | 6 oz milk chocolate
6 wooden sticks

METHOD:

Toast the hazelnuts lightly in a dry pan then transfer to a deep plate.

Insert a wooden stick into each apple.

Melt the chocolate over simmering water. Do not stir, but mix lightly with a fork at the end to give a marbled effect.

Dip the apples one after the other into the melted chocolate and coat evenly.

Finally dip the apples into the chopped nuts, turning and pressing the nuts into the chocolate. Leave to set.

Chocolate petit fours with marzipan

Prep and cook time: 45 minutes * Cannot be frozen * Makes: 24

INGREDIENTS:

250 g | 9 oz | 2 cups plain|all purpose

1 tbsp cocoa powder

50 g | 1 ¾ oz dark chocolate, very finely chopped, or grated

1 tsp baking powder

½ tsp baking soda

1 egg

120 g | 4 oz | ⅗ cup sugar

125 g | 4 ½ oz | 1 stick softened butter

300 g | 11 oz | 1 ⅓ cup sour cream

200 g | 7 oz marzipan paste, cut into 24 pieces

For the frosting:

180 g | 6 oz milk chocolate

250 g | 9 oz | 1 cup cream cheese

1 tbsp milk

50 g | ¾ oz icing |confectioners' sugar

METHOD:

Heat the oven to 200°C (180°C fan) 400°F, gas 6 and place the paper cases in the muffin pan.

Mix the flour with the cocoa, grated chocolate, baking powder and baking soda.

Beat the egg in a large bowl. Add the sugar, butter and sour cream and mix well.

Add the flour mixture and mix until everything is just combined.

Fill each paper case to just less than half with the mixture, press a piece of marzipan in the centre and top off with more mixture.

Bake for 20 minutes, remove from the oven, rest for 5 minutes then remove from the muffin pan and cool on a wire rack.

For the frosting, melt the chocolate over simmering water, remove from the heat and let cool. Mix in the cream cheese, milk and icing/confectioners' sugar and frost the petit fours. Leave in a cool place to set.

Macaroons with chocolate coffee cream

Prep and cook time: 45 minutes * Cannot be frozen * Makes: 20 - 25

INGREDIENTS:

200 g | 7 oz | 2 cups ground almonds
100 g | 3 ½ oz | ½ cup sugar
2 egg whites
icing|confectioners' sugar to dust

For the filling:
100 g | 3 ½ oz dark chocolate, 70% cocoa
50 ml | 1 ¾ fl oz | 10 tsp cream
1 tsp instant coffee

METHOD:

Heat the oven to 150°C (130°C fan) 300°F, gas 2.

Mix the almonds with half the sugar.

Beat the egg whites with the remaining sugar until very stiff and glossy.

Carefully fold the almond mixture into the egg whites and spoon into a piping bag with a plain nozzle.

Pipe 40 - 45 small heaps of the mixture (approximately 0.5") onto a cookie sheet lined with baking parchment, dust with icing/confectioners' sugar and bake for 15 minutes. Switch off the oven and let the macaroons cool in the oven.

Meanwhile, melt the chocolate over simmering water, remove from heat and allow to cool.

Warm the cream slightly and dissolve the instant coffee in it. Allow the coffee cream cool and then whip until stiff.

Fold the coffee cream into the cold melted chocolate.

Spread the chocolate filling onto half of the macaroons, top with the remaining halves, press to firm and serve dusted with icing/confectioners' sugar.

Marshmallow ice cream cake

Prep and cook time: 40 minutes ∗ Freezing time: 4 hours ∗ Can be frozen ∗ Serves: 8 - 10

INGREDIENTS:

For the base:
200 g | 7 oz | ½ cup digestive biscuits
80 g | 3 oz | 6 tbsp butter, melted
2 tbsp sugar

For the ice cream:
100 g | 3 ½ oz | 2 cups mini marshmallows, finely chopped
750 ml | 26 fl oz | 3 cups milk
1 lemon, zest finely grated
5 egg yolks
125 g | 4 ½ oz | 10 tbsp sugar
5 tbsp grated dark chocolate

To decorate:
250 ml | 9 fl oz | 1 cup cream
100 g | 3 ½ oz milk chocolate
mini marshmallows

METHOD:

Mix together the butter, crushed cookies and sugar. Tip the mixture into a 23 cm | 9 in tart pan and press down firmly, forming a border around the edge about 0.5" high. Place the base in the refrigerator to chill.

To make the ice cream, bring the milk to a boil and remove from the heat.

Beat the egg yolks and sugar until pale and creamy. Slowly pour into the warm milk, stirring to combine.

Return the mixture to the heat and cook until creamy, stirring constantly (do not allow to boil). Add the lemon zest and allow to cool, stirring occasionally.

Stir in the grated chocolate and chopped marshmallows.

Place in the freezer for 3 hours, beating well every 30 minutes.

Spread the marshmallow ice cream onto the cold base in the shape of a dome and freeze for a further hour until the ice cream is solid.

Before serving, whip the cream softly and spread over the ice cream cake, beginning in the middle of the dome and working outwards.

Remove the cake from the cake pan and cut into slices. Carefully lift the slices using a cake slice and arrange on dessert plates.

Melt the chocolate and drizzle over the cake slices. Garnish with mini marshmallows to serve.

Chocolate liqueur with chocolate thins

Prep and cook time: 30 minutes * Cannot be frozen * Serves: 4

INGREDIENTS:

For the liqueur:
250 g | 9 oz milk chocolate
300 ml | 11 fl oz | 1 ⅓ cups cream
1 dl | 3 tbsp coffee liqueur
ice cubes

For the chocolate thins:
100 g | 3 ½ oz milk chocolate,
finely chopped
1 tbsp icing|confectioners' sugar
25 g | 1 oz | 3 tbsp silver sugar

METHOD:

To make the liqueur, place the chocolate in a pan with the cream and melt slowly over a low heat.

Allow it to cool and pour into a shaker along with the coffee liqueur and 5 ice cubes and shake well.

Divide between 4 glasses filled with ice.

To make the chocolate thins, melt the chocolate over simmering water, let cool slightly, pour onto baking parchment and smooth.

Let them set slightly and then cut out shapes with a round cookie cutter (8 cm in diameter). Leave to set completely.

To decorate, mix the icing/confectioners' sugar with a little water to a thick consistency. Pipe onto the chocolate thins in lines and sprinkle with silver sugar.

Hazelnut fancy with chocolate cream

Prep and cook time: 30 minutes ∗ Cannot be frozen ∗ Makes: 4

INGREDIENTS:

½ vanilla pod
125 ml | 4 ½ fl oz | ½ cup milk
75 g | 2 ½ oz dark chocolate, 70 % cocoa
60 g | 2 oz | ½ stick butter
60 g | 2 oz | ½ cup plain|
all purpose flour
4 egg whites
4 egg yolks
30 g | 1 oz | ⅓ cup ground roasted
hazelnuts (cob nuts)
50 g | 1 ¾ oz | ¼ cup sugar
butter and sugar for the moulds
nut liqueur

To decorate:
150 g | 5 oz dark chocolate, 70 % cocoa
3 tbsp chocolate hazelnut spread
75 g | 2 ½ oz | ⅓ cup cream
100 g | 3 ½ oz | ½ cup toasted chopped
hazelnuts (cob nuts)

METHOD:

Heat the oven to 180°C (160°C fan) 375°F, gas 5.

Slit the vanilla pod lengthways and scrape out the seeds. Heat the milk, the vanilla pod and the vanilla seeds in a saucepan.

Melt the dark chocolate over simmering of hot water.

Melt the butter in a saucepan. Add the flour and stir until the paste is smooth. Remove the vanilla pod from the milk and pour into the butter paste. Simmer for 10 minutes, stirring occasionally.

Pour the mixture into a mixing bowl and let cool slightly. Stir in two unbeaten egg whites, followed by the egg yolks, one after the other stirring the mixture until smooth.

Pour in the melted chocolate and add the ground hazelnuts.Whisk the two remaining egg whites with the sugar until stiff.

Stir ¼ of the egg whites into the batter using a whisk, then careful fold in the remaining egg white.

Butter the 4 x 225 ml | 8 fl oz moulds and sprinkle with sugar.

Fill the moulds with the batter until ¾ full using a piping bag with large nozzle.

Place the moulds in a roasting pan half-filled with water and bake in for 25 - 30 minutes.

Turn out of the moulds and let cool.

Pour a drop of nut liqueur over the fancies, according to taste.

To decorate, melt the chopped dark chocolate, chocolate hazelnut spread and the cream, then let cool. Cover the cakes with the chocolate spread, sprinkle some roasted hazelnuts over the top and serve.

Chocolate profiteroles with chocolate cream

Prep and cook time: 50 minutes * Cannot be frozen * Makes: 20

INGREDIENTS:

60 g | 1 ¾ oz | ½ stick butter

1 tbsp sugar

1 pinch salt

180 g | 6 oz | 1 ½ cups plain|
all purpose flour

1 tsp baking powder

4 eggs

1 tbsp cocoa powder

For the filling:

250 ml | 9 fl oz | 1 cup cream

1 vanilla pod

4 egg yolks

100 g | 3 ½ oz | ½ cup sugar

250 g | 9 oz | 2 ¼ sticks butter,
room temperature

150 g | 5 oz dark chocolate, 70% cocoa

METHOD:

Heat the oven to 200°C (180°C fan) 400°F, gas 6.

To make the choux pastry, bring 250 ml (1 cup) of water to a boil with the butter, sugar and salt.

Pour in all the flour in, add the cocoa powder and stir vigorously over a low heat until the dough forms a ball and leaves the sides of the pan clean.

Tip the dough into a bowl and beat in the eggs one at a time. Finally, beat in the baking powder.

Fill a piping bag with the choux pastry and pipe 20 walnut-sized cookies onto a cookie tray lined with baking parchment. Bake for 25 minutes.

Remove from the oven and slice each profiterole through horizontally. Replace the pastry lids and let cool.

To make the filling, split the vanilla pod and place in a pan with the cream. Bring the cream to a boil, remove from the heat and leave to steep.

Beat the egg yolk and sugar until thick and creamy and stir in the hot cream. Pour back into the pan and cook over a medium heat stirring with a spatula, do not let the mixture boil.

Push the sauce through a sieve and let cool down to room temperature.

Beat the butter with an electric whisk until pale and fluffy then whisk the vanilla cream into the butter little by little. Melt the chocolate over simmering water, let cool and mix into the cream.

Spoon the filing into a piping bag with a large star nozzle. Pipe a portion onto the bottom half of each profiterole and replace the top.

Cherries in white chocolate and coconut

Prep and cook time: 35 minutes * Soaking time: 48 hours * Cannot be frozen * Makes: 50

INGREDIENTS:

50 sweet cherries with stalks, washed and drained, stalks intact

250 ml | 9 fl oz | 1 cup cognac

250 g | 9 oz white chocolate

150 g | 5 oz | 1 ½ cups shredded (desiccated) coconut

METHOD:

Place the cherries in a bowl and pour over the cognac. Cover and leave to soak for at least 2 days in the refrigerator. The cherries should be covered by the cognac at all times (add more cognac if necessary).

Drain the cherries and pat well dry.

Melt the chocolate over simmering water.

Hold the cherries by their stalks and dip into the chocolate, allowing any excess to drip off.

Place on a wire rack or baking parchment to set slightly, then roll in the shredded coconut and leave to set completely.

Yufka tarts with berries and chocolate

Prep and cook time: 45 minutes * Cannot be frozen * Makes: 12

INGREDIENTS:

400 g | 14 oz yufka pastry sheets
(filo pastry can be used as a substitute)
egg white
butter, to grease the pan
200 g | 7 oz | 1 ⅓ cup mixed berries,
washed and prepared

For the filling:
150 g | 5 oz dark chocolate, 70% cocoa
400 ml milk
1 vanilla pod
40 g | 1 ½ oz | ⅓ cup cornflour|cornstarch
4 egg yolks
4 tbsp sugar

METHOD:

Heat the oven to 220°C (200°C fan) 425°F, gas 7.

Brush each pastry sheet with a little beaten egg white and layer in stacks of 4 sheets. Do not brush to top layer with egg white. From the layered pastry, cut out 12 squares about 10 cm along each side.

Butter the cups of a muffin tin.

Lay the pastry squares in the muffin tin cups and bake for 10 minutes until crispy. Remove from the pan and allow to cool.

To make the filling, melt a third of the chocolate and spread thinly onto a hard, cold surface. Leave until completely hardened then scrape off with a spatula and reserve for the garnish.

Pour the milk into a pan, reserving 3 tbsp. Heat the milk with the vanilla pod and remaining chocolate.

Remove the vanilla pod, mix the cornflour/cornstarch to a paste with the reserved milk and add to the chocolate milk. Bring briefly to a boil and remove from the heat.

Beat the egg yolks and sugar in a metal bowl over simmering water until creamy. Slowly pour in the chocolate milk and beat again until thick and creamy.

Let the filling cool, stirring occasionally, and spoon into the pastry cases.

Divide the berries between the tarts and garnish with the shaved chocolate curls.

Chocolate mousse bars

Prep and cook time: 1 hour * Setting time: 3 hours * Cannot be frozen * Makes: 30 bars

INGREDIENTS:

For the sponge cake:
5 eggs, separated
125 g | 4 1/2 oz | 2/3 cup sugar
100 g | 3 1/2 oz | 1/5 cup plain|
all purpose flour
50 g | 1 3/4 oz | 1/2 cup cornflour|cornstarch

For the mousse:
150 g | 5 oz dark chocolate
2 eggs, separated
40 g | 1 1/2 oz | 1/5 cup sugar
75 g | 2 1/2 oz cream, whipped

For the frosting:
200 g | 7 oz dark chocolate,
broken into pieces
200 g | 7 oz | 1 cup sugar

Also:
200 g | 7 oz | 1 1/2 cups mixed nuts, peeled
almonds and peanuts, roughly chopped
4 tbsp sugar

METHOD:

Heat the oven to 220°C (200°C fan) 425°F, gas 7.

To make the sponge cake, whisk the egg whites until stiff. Beat the egg yolks with the sugar until pale and creamy.Mix together flour and cornflour/cornstarch. Alternately fold the egg yolks and flour mixture into the beaten egg whites.

Line a cookie sheet with baking parchment and spread with the mixture. Bake for around 15 minutes until golden brown.

Remove from the oven and let it cool. Cut into two halves lengthways.

To make the mousse, melt the chocolate over a pan of simmering water, remove from the heat and let cool.

Whisk the egg whites with half the sugar until they form stiff peaks.

Beat the egg yolks with the remaining sugar over simmering water until the sugar has completely dissolved. Remove from the heat and continue beating until cooled. Pour the egg yolk mixture into the chocolate and whisk to combine.

Pour the whipped cream onto the chocolate and fold in using a whisk. Carefully fold in the egg whites little by little.

Spread the mousse onto one sponge cake and lay the second sponge on top. Press gently to firm and put the sponge into the fridge to chill. Once it is cool, slice into finger-sized pieces.

To make the frosting, heat the sugar, 125 ml (5/8 cup) water and the chocolate in a pan. Simmer for 5 minutes, stirring constantly and let cool, still stirring.

Caramelise the sugar in a non-stick pan until golden brown. Mix in the nuts, allow to cool on baking parchment and crumble.

Dip the mousse bars into the cooled frosting, scatter with the caramelised nuts and allow to cool for at least 3 hours.

Chocolate pralines

Prep and cook time: 45 minutes * Setting time: 3 hours * Cannot be frozen * Makes: 30

INGREDIENTS:

300 g | 11 oz dark chocolate,
roughly chopped
200 ml | 7 fl oz | ⅞ cup cream
250 ml | 9 fl oz | 1 cup advocaat liqueur
600 g | 21 oz milk chocolate
30 milk chocolate hollow praline shells

METHOD:

Place the chopped dark chocolate into a bowl.

Bring the cream to a boil and stir into the chocolate little by little using a spatula. Take care not to mix too much air into the chocolate. Let cool slightly.

Using a piston funnel, fill the hollow shells to ⅓ with advocaat.

Spoon the chocolate mixture into a piping bag and fill the shells to just below the rim. Leave to set for at least 2 hours.

Melt 100 g of the milk chocolate over simmering water, let cool slightly and spoon into a fine piping bag. Use the chocolate to stick the chocolate shells together and leave to set.

Melt the remaining chocolate and let cool slightly.

Using a praline fork, dip the pralines into the chocolate coating and lay on a cooling rack. When the coating has set slightly, gently roll the pralines from side to side on the rack to create a decorative surface. Place on baking parchment and leave to set completely.

Mocha choc macaroons

Prep and cook time: 45 minutes * Cannot be frozen * Makes: 60

INGREDIENTS:

3 egg whites
100 g | 3 ½ oz | ½ cup sugar
300 g | 11 oz | 3 cups ground almonds
100 g | 3 ½ oz dark chocolate
2 tsp instant coffee
50 g | 1 ¾ oz | ⅖ cup plain|
all purpose flour
60 rice-paper circles
150 g | 5 oz white chocolate, chopped
2 tbsp crème fraiche

To garnish:
60 chocolate mocha beans

METHOD:

Heat the oven to 180°C (160°C fan) 375°F, gas mark 5.

Beat the egg whites in a large bowl with the sugar until they form stiff peaks.

Mix together the almonds, chocolate, coffee and flour and fold into the egg whites.

Spoon the mixture into a piping bag with a smooth nozzle. Place the rice-paper circles onto a cookie sheet and pipe a little macaroon on top of each.

Bake the macaroons for 20 - 25 minutes until golden brown and let cool.

Melt the white chocolate and crème fraiche over simmering water, allow the mixture to cool and then place half a teaspoon on each macaroon. Top each dab with a mocha bean and leave to set.

Chocolate fingers

Prep and cook time: 1 hour * Chill: 1 hour * Cannot be frozen * Makes: 50 - 60

INGREDIENTS:

For the dough:

125 g | 4 ½ oz dark chocolate, 70% cocoa
125 g | 4 ½ oz | 1 stick softened butter
175 g | 6 oz | 1 cup icing|confectioners'
sugar
100 g | 3 ½ oz | 1 ¾ cup peeled hazelnuts
(cob nuts)
100 g | 3 ½ oz | 1 cup ground almonds
20 g | ¾ oz | ⅕ cup flour
20 g | ¾ oz | 2 tbsp
cornflour|cornstarch
1 tbsp cocoa powder

For the dark fingers:

50 ml | 1 ¾ fl oz | 10 tsp cream
1 pinch ground cinnamon
100 g | 3 ½ oz milk chocolate
75 g | 2 ½ oz dark chocolate, 75% cocoa

For the light fingers:

75 g | 2 ½ oz white chocolate
20 g | ¾ oz milk chocolate

METHOD:

To make the dough, melt the dark chocolate over simmering water and let cool slightly. Beat the butter and icing/confectioners' sugar to a creamy consistency and stir into the liquid chocolate. In a food processor, grind the hazelnuts quite finely, but not to a powder.

Mix together the hazelnuts, almonds, cornflour/cornstarch and cocoa powder and quickly work into the chocolate mixture to make a dough. Halve the dough, wrap in plastic wrap and chill for 1 hour.

Heat the oven to 160°C (140°C fan) 325°F, gas 3.

For the dark cookie filling, heat the cream with the cinnamon. Dissolve the milk chocolate in the cream and let it cool.

Remove one dough portion from the refrigerator and roll out to 5 mm thick on a floured work surface. Use a knife to cut out the dough into sticks 1.5 x 5 cm.

Roll out the dough for the light cookies on a floured surface, to roughly the same size.

Place all of the sticks onto baking trays and bake for 15 minutes until golden brown. Remove from the baking trays and let cool.

To fill the darker sticks, beat the cold chocolate cream until smooth. Spread on half of the sticks, top with the remaining halves and press down gently.

To decorate the darker sticks, melt the chocolate over simmering water. Dip the sticks half into the chocolate at an angle and leave to set.

To decorate the smaller sticks, melt the white chocolate over simmering water. Dip in the sticks by one third and leave to set on baking parchment. Melt the milk chocolate and drizzle over the white chocolate. Leave to set.

Marbled chocolate meringues

Prep and cook time: 1 hour * Cannot be frozen * Makes: 20 meringues

INGREDIENTS:

100 g | 3 ½ oz dark chocolate
5 egg whites
200 g | 7 oz | 1 ¼ cup icing|
confectioners' sugar
1 pinch salt

Also:
baking parchment

METHOD:

Heat the oven to 140°C (120°C fan) 275°F, gas 1.

Break up the chocolate and melt it in a bowl over simmering water.

For the meringue, mix the egg whites with the icing/confectioners' sugar and salt. Then whisk until stiff over simmering water until the temperature reaches about 50°C. Remove from the heat and slowly beat the egg whites until cold.

Drizzle the chocolate over the beaten egg whites and fold in with a rubber spatula until the egg white is slightly marbled.

Spoon the meringue mixture onto a baking tray lined with baking parchment, making about 20 meringues.

Bake for 35 - 40 minutes until the meringues are crisp on the outside but still soft inside. Leave to cool.

Christmas petit fours

Prep and cook time: 1 hour * Waiting time: 2 hours * Cannot be frozen * Makes: 35

INGREDIENTS:

For the sponge cake:

5 eggs, separated

125 g | 4 ½ oz | ½ cup sugar

50 g | 1 ¾ oz | ½ stick butter, melted

75 g | 2 ½ oz | ⅔ cup plain|
all purpose flour

50 g | 1 ¾ oz | ½ cup
cornflour|cornstarch

50 g | 1 ¾ oz | ½ cup ground almonds

For the filling:

4 cl | 3 tbsp rum

100 g | 3 ½ oz | ⅓ cup apricot jam (jelly)

For the frosting:

600 g | 21 oz marzipan

50 g | 1 ¾ oz | ½ cup icing|
confectioners' sugar

a few drops of yellow food coloring

2 - 3 tbsp cream

sugar beads for decorating

METHOD:

Heat the oven to 220°C (200°C fan) 425°F, gas 7.

To make the sponge cake, beat the egg yolks and sugar until creamy and thick. Beat the egg whites until stiff and fold into the egg yolks along with the melted butter, flour, cornflour/cornstarch and almonds.

Spread the batter out thinly on a cookie sheet lined with baking parchment and bake for 12 minutes until golden brown. Turn onto a cooling rack, peel off the baking parchment, cover and allow to cool for at least 2 hours.

Cut the sponge cake into quarters with a sharp knife and drizzle with rum.

Warm the jam, stirring constantly, and push through a sieve.

Brush the sponge cakes with about ⅔ of the jam, cut into approximately 35 cubes and brush the sides with the remaining jam.

To make the frosting, knead the marzipan thoroughly with the icing/confectioners' sugar and food coloring. Roll out on a work surface dusted with icing/confectioners' sugar and cut out circles. The circles' diameter should be about 3 times the height of the petit fours.

Lay the marzipan circles on the petit fours, trim the edges and mould into shape. Scraps can be kneaded together and rolled out again.

To decorate, mix 4 tbsp confectioner's sugar with the cream to a thick consistency and pipe patterns onto the petit fours with a very fine nozzle. Decorate with sugar beads.

Chocolate chilli truffles

Prep and cook time: 40 minutes Waiting time: 2 hours * Cannot be frozen * Makes: 25 - 30

INGREDIENTS:

1 red chili pepper, rinsed, cleaned, slit
lengthways, deseeded and very
finely chopped
200 g | 7 oz dark chocolate, 70% cocoa
100 g | 3 ½ oz | ½ cup crème fraiche
3 tbsp cognac
1 tbsp butter
4 tbsp cocoa powder

METHOD:

Heat the crème fraiche, add the chocolate and stir until dissolved.

Stir in the chilli, cognac and butter and chill until the mixture is firm
but not solid, about 2 hours.

Scoop out teaspoonfuls of the truffle mixture and use your hands
to quickly roll into balls.

Roll the truffles in cocoa powder and then roll across a wire rack
to pattern the surface.

Serve in paper cases if desired.

Orange tartlets with white chocolate mousse

Prep and cook time: 50 minutes * Chill: 3 hours * Cannot be frozen * Makes: 12

INGREDIENTS:

For the short crust pastry:
200 g | 7 oz | 1 ½ cups plain|
all purpose flour
100 g | 3 ½ oz | 1 stick butter
70 g | 2 ½ oz ¾ cup icing|
confectioners' sugar
1 good pinch salt
1 egg yolk
1 tbsp milk
100 g | 3 ½ oz milk chocolate

For the mousse:
5 leaves of gelatine, soaked in cold water
2 eggs
2 egg yolks
50 g | 1 ¾ oz | ¼ cup sugar
2 cl | 1 ½ tbsp white rum
350 g | 12 oz white chocolate
400 ml | 14 fl oz | 1 ⅔ cups cream
4 oranges
2 cl | 1 ½ tbsp orange liqueur
1 tbsp honey
icing|confectioners' sugar to dust

METHOD:

Heat the oven to 200°C (180°C fan) 400°F, gas 6.

To make the pastry, combine the flour, butter, icing/confectioners' sugar, salt, egg yolks and milk to form a dough. Wrap in cling film and chill for 30 minutes.

Roll the dough out to 3 - 4 mm (⅛ ") thickness and use to line 12 tartlet or bun pans. Bake for 15 minutes until golden brown.

Carefully remove from the pans and allow to cool.

Melt the milk chocolate over simmering water and brush the inside of the pastry cases with chocolate. Leave to cool.

To make the mousse, beat the eggs, egg yolks, sugar and rum over simmering water (do not allow to boil).

Melt the white chocolate and stir into the egg mixture.

Squeeze the gelatine to remove excess water, mix into the egg mixture and allow to cool slightly.

Whip the cream until stiff.

Once the chocolate mixture has begun to thicken, fold in the whipped cream and spoon into a piping bag.

Pipe the filling into the tartlets and chill for at least 2 hours.

Chocolate muesli cookies

Prep and cook time: 30 minutes * Cannot be frozen * Makes: 20 - 25 cookies

INGREDIENTS:

150 g | 5 oz | 1 ⅕ cups mixed nuts
(almonds, pecans, pistachios
and walnuts)
50 g | 1 ¾ oz | ⅔ cup rolled oats
2 tbsp brown sugar
1 tbsp honey
350 g | 12 oz dark chocolate, 70% cocoa
150 g | 5 oz milk chocolate
10 g | ¼ oz | 1 tbsp coconut oil

METHOD:

Place the nuts and rolled oats in a food processor and chop roughly.

Caramelise the sugar and honey in a pan and stir in the nut mixture.

Spread the mixture out on baking parchment, let it cool and crumble
into pieces.

Melt the chocolate with the coconut oil over simmering water. Let
cool slightly and then spoon onto silicon paper in portions (2 tbsp).

Leave to set slightly, scatter with the muesli mixture and leave
to cool completely.

Chocolate Christmas puddings

Prep and cook time: 1 hour 15 minutes * Chill: 2 hours * Cannot be frozen * Makes: 4

INGREDIENTS:

For the sponge base:

2 eggs

50 g | 1 ¾ oz | ¼ cup sugar

½ tbsp vanilla extract

50 g | 1 ¾ oz | 8 tbsp plain|
all purpose flour

½ tbsp cornflour|cornstarch

2 tbsp cocoa powder

For the chocolate mixture:

50 g | 1 ¾ oz | ¼ cup quark
(low-fat soft cheese)

50 g | 1 ¾ oz | ¼ cup crème fraiche,
low-fat

50 g | 1 ¾ oz dark chocolate, melted

75 g | 2 ½ oz marzipan, grated

25 g | 1 oz | 2 tbsp sugar

1 cl | 2 tsp rum

50 ml | 1 ¾ fl oz | 10 tsp cream

Decoration:

cocoa powder for rolling

40 g | 1 ½ oz marzipan paste

10 g | ¼ oz | 1 ½ tbsp icing|
confectioners' sugar

red and green food colouring

icing|confectioners' sugar to dust

METHOD:

Heat the oven to 180°C (160°C fan) 375°F, gas 5.

Spray a baking tray with a little water and line with baking parchment.

Beat the egg yolks with 2 tbsp warm water and half of the sugar and the vanilla extract until foamy.

In a separate bowl, whisk the egg whites, trickling in the rest of the sugar before they are completely stiff. Then continue beating until stiff. Fold the beaten egg whites into the egg yolk mixture with a spoon.

Mix the flour with the cornflour/cornstarch and cocoa and sieve over the mixture, then fold it in. Spread the mixture evenly on the prepared baking tray and bake for 10 - 12 minutes.

When done, take out of the oven and turn on to a tea towel sprinkled with sugar. Pull off the baking parchment, cover the sponge with a damp dish towel and let cool. Cut the sponge into small cubes.

Melt the dark chocolate and allow to cool.

Mix together the quark, crème fraiche, cooled chocolate, marzipan, sugar and rum.

Whip the cream until stiff and fold into the chocolate cream.

Add the pieces of sponge and stir to produce a smooth mixture (add a little more cream if necessary).

Form the mixture into 4 balls, roll in cocoa and chill.

To decorate, knead the marzipan with the icing/confectioners' sugar. Colour one half of the marzipan with red food colouring and roll into small balls for the berries. Colour the second half green and shape into holly leaves. Before serving, dust the 'Christmas puddings' with a little icing/confectioners' sugar and add the marzipan leaves and berries.

Chocolate gingerbread hearts

Prep and cook time: 1 hour * Chill: 12 hours * Cannot be frozen * Makes: 50

INGREDIENTS:

For the dough:
250 g | 9 oz | ¾ cup honey
250 g | 9 oz | 1 ¼ cups cane sugar
150 g | 5 oz | 1 ½ sticks butter
2 eggs
100 g | 3 ½ oz | 1 cup ground almonds
400 g | 14 oz | 3 ½ cups plain|
all purpose flour
1 tsp ground cinnamon
2 tsp gingerbread spice
1 tsp grated lemon zest
1 tbsp cocoa
1 tsp baking (bicarbonate of) soda
2 cl rum

For the coating:
250 g | 9 oz dark chocolate
3 tbsp cream
sugar hearts for decoration

METHOD:

To make the dough, heat the honey, cane sugar and butter in a pan, stirring constantly, until the sugar has dissolved. Pour into a large mixing bowl and allow to cool.

Add the eggs, almonds, flour, cinnamon, gingerbread spices, lemon zest and cocoa to the sugar mixture and knead thoroughly using the dough hook of the kitchen mixer.

Mix the baking soda with the rum and add to the dough. Continue kneading until the dough is glossy and leaves the bowl clean.
Add a little more flour if necessary.

Cover the bowl with tin foil and place in the refrigerator overnight.

Heat the oven to 180°C (160°C fan) 375°F, gas 5.

Roll the dough out in portions on a floured work surface to just under ½ inch thick and cut out heart shapes.

Lay the gingerbread hearts on a cookie sheet lined with baking parchment and bake for 15 - 20 minutes.

Carefully remove from the cookie sheet (the hearts will still be very soft) and allow to cool completely.

To make the coating, melt the chocolate with the cream over simmering water. Stir well, remove from the heat and allow to cool slightly.

Using a praline fork, dip the hearts into the coating, let any excess drip off and place the hearts onto a wire rack to dry.

Use any remaining chocolate to decorate the hearts (reheating if necessary) and sprinkle with sugar hearts.

Chocolate macaroons with fig filling

Prep and cook time: 50 minutes * Cannot be frozen * Makes: 25 - 30

INGREDIENTS:

3 egg whites
1 tsp lemon juice
1 pinch salt
200 g | 7 oz | 1 cup sugar
200 g | 7 oz | 2 cups almonds, peeled and ground
2 tbsp cornflour|cornstarch
2 tbsp cocoa powder
1/2 tsp ground cinnamon

For the filling:
100 g | 3 ½ oz marzipan, finely grated
200 g | 7 oz | 1 ¼ cups dried figs
1 - 2 tbsp almond liqueur

METHOD:

Heat the oven to 170°C (150°C fan) 350°F, gas 4.

Beat the egg whites with the lemon juice, salt and sugar until all the sugar has dissolved and the egg whites are glossy and form very stiff peaks.

Mix together the almonds, cornflour/cornstarch, cocoa powder and cinnamon and fold carefully into the egg whites.

Spoon the mixture into a piping bag with a large nozzle and pipe around 50-60 small piles (1.5" in size) onto a cookie sheet lined with baking parchment at 1.25" intervals.

Bake the macaroons for 25 - 30 minutes and remove from the oven. Lift the macaroons from the cookie sheet immediately and cool on a wire rack.

To make the filling, place the figs and liqueur in a food processor and puree.

Scrape the figs into a bowl with the grated marzipan and mix well.

Divide the fig marzipan into 25 - 30 pieces, roll into balls and flatten slightly.

Place each piece of fig marzipan between two macaroons and press together gently.

Chocolate meringues

Prep and cook time: 1 hour 15 minutes * Cannot be frozen * Makes: 30

INGREDIENTS:

4 egg whites
2 tsp lemon juice
250 g | 9 oz | 2 ½ cups icing|
confectioners' sugar
1 tsp cocoa powder

For the filling:
100 g | 3 ½ oz dark chocolate, 70% cocoa
2 tbsp cream
20 g | ¾ oz | ¼ stick butter
1 tbsp kirsch

METHOD:

Heat the oven to 130°C (110°C fan) 250°F, gas 2.

Beat the egg whites with the lemon juice until very stiff. Add the cocoa powder and icing/confectioners' sugar little by little and continue beating until the mixture is firm and glossy.

Spoon the mixture into a piping bag with a large round nozzle. Pipe small meringues about 1 inch onto a cookie sheet lined with baking parchment.

Bake the meringues for 50 - 60 minutes in the preheated oven, making sure they do not burn.

To make the filling, carefully melt the chocolate over simmering water. Remove from the heat and whisk in the cream and the butter in small flakes.

Stir in the kirsch and let cool.

Spread half the meringues with the chocolate filling and assemble using the remaining meringues.

Stracciatella mousse in chocolate shells

Prep and cook time: 25 minutes ∗ Chill: 1 hour ∗ Cannot be frozen ∗ Makes: 20

INGREDIENTS:

For the shells:
250 g | 9 oz dark chocolate

For the filling:
200 g | 7 oz | 1 cup mascarpone
200 g | 7 oz | 1 cup yoghurt
200 g | 7 oz | 1 cup quark
(low-fat soft cheese)
2 tbsp lemon juice
4 cl | 3 tbsp white rum
1 good pinch vanilla pod seeds
100 g | 3 ½ oz | 1 cup icing|
confectioners' sugar
300 ml | 11 fl oz | 1 ⅓ cups cream
50 g | 1 ¾ oz dark chocolate

METHOD:

To make the shells, melt the chocolate over simmering water.

Allow to cool slightly and pour into small silicon baking cups (approximately 2.5" in diameter). Tip each cup to ensure even coverage of surfaces until the chocolate begins to set. Smooth the top edges and leave to set completely.

When completely cold, remove from the silicon cups.

To make the filling, mix the mascarpone, yoghurt, quark, lemon juice, rum, vanilla seeds and icing/confectioners' sugar to a smooth consistency.

Whip the cream until stiff and fold into the mascarpone along with the grated chocolate.

Spoon the mixture into a piping bag with a smooth nozzle and pipe into the chocolate shells.

Chill for at least 1 hour and serve.

White chocolate truffles

Prep and cook time: 40 minutes * Chill: 2 hours * Cannot be frozen * Makes: 35 - 40

INGREDIENTS:

200 g | 7 oz dark chocolate, 70% cocoa
100 g | 3 ½ oz | ½ cup crème fraiche
3 tbsp rum
1 tbsp butter
4 tbsp cocoa powder
300 g | 11 oz white chocolate

METHOD:

To make the truffle filling, heat the crème fraiche, add the dark chocolate and stir until melted. Stir in the rum and butter and remove from the heat.

Chill until the mixture has firmed but is not solid, after about an hour.

Use your hands to roll small portions of the mixture into balls and chill again for 20 minutes.

To coat the truffles, melt the white chocolate over simmering water and let cool slightly.

Dip the truffles into the white chocolate using a praline fork and place on a wire rack or baking parchment to set.

INDEX.

INDEX.

INDEX.